DAYDREAMING

STUDIES IN
PSYCHOLOGY

Consulting Editor:

L. JOSEPH STONE

Vassar College

DAYDREAMING

*An Introduction
to the Experimental Study of
Inner Experience*

BY

JEROME L. SINGER

The City College of The City University of New York

&

*Center for Research in Cognition and Affect
The City University of New York*

RANDOM HOUSE

New York

To Dorothy

Foreword

This work presents a new conception of the nature of daydreaming. It is at once a consequence of and an important contribution to a radical transformation in our understanding of the nature of man.

For several decades now "behavior" and unconscious hydraulic-like forces have dominated the study of the human being. The human being was conceived either as an empty organism controlled by stimulus conditions or as an organism controlled essentially by states of drive deficit.

In recent years psychoanalytic theory has been tempered by the emergence of ego psychology. The dominance of drive theory and stimulus control theory has waned in the face of the rise of cognitive theory and affect theory, and of developments in neurophysiology and in computer simulation. The paradox of this second half of the twentieth century is that the return to the classical problems of attention and consciousness is not a return by psychologists who have had a change of heart. It is a derivative, rather, of the initiative of the neurophysiologists and the automata designers. The neurophysiologists boldly entered the site of consciousness with electrodes and amplifiers. They found that the stream of consciousness from the past could be turned on and off by appropriate stimulation. They found that there were amplifier structures which could be turned up and down by drugs and by electrical stimulation, and that consciousness varied as a function of such manipulation. They found that seizures and the loss of consciousness were a consequence of excessive stimulation of cortical and subcortical circuitry. They found that there were filter networks which appeared to prevent consciousness by attenuation of sensory input at or near the sensory receptors themselves.

The renewed interest in consciousness and in cognition in general is a consequence also of the extraordinary capabilities of the computer. Thinking as a psychological phenomenon gained respectability and credibility when it was demonstrated that computers could be programmed to simulate complex thought processes—that they could pay attention to input—consult their past experience—consider alternatives and make intelligent decisions—in short, that they could mimic the designers who intended they should do so.

Neither the brain as revealed by contemporary neurophysiology nor the brain as simulated by the modern high speed computer gave any support or comfort to the simplistic conceptions of the nature of the human being which had dominated American psychology for the past thirty years.

It now appears that the organism is neither empty nor simple-minded. Impressive as are the capabilities of the modern computer, they have thrown into relief the hitherto unappreciated capacities of the human brain as an information processing mechanism. Further, the conceptualization and quantification of the idea of information permitted a rough estimation of the relative magnitudes of human information processing capabilities.

The theory of automata introduced not only the idea of information, but also the conception of a feedback mechanism in which a predetermined state is achieved by utilizing information about the difference between the achieved state and the predetermined state to reduce this difference to zero. The thermostat is a familiar example. As the reading of the thermometer goes above a chosen setting, the fuel supply to the furnace is progressively reduced. As its reading falls below that setting, the fuel flow is increased. A predetermined temperature is maintained by using the amount and direction of departure from the desired condition as a signal to activate the control mechanism in a compensatory manner. The significance of the application of this engineering conception to psychology was profound. It could no longer be comfortably maintained that the concept of "purpose," which dealt with the non-existent future, was scientifically untenable.

The application of the idea of a feedback system governed by stored complex information also revolutionized microbiology and genetics. The genetic code by which life is maintained and reproduced is now being decoded. Here too the most complex biological processes have turned out to be governed by "information" stored not in the brain, but in the genes.

The emergence of the theory of cognition and the belated awareness of the informational capabilities of man was the first half of the revolution. The second half of the revolution concerns the nature of human motivation. If man can think better than we supposed

—what does he think *about*? Up to and including
Freud and Hull the answer was: his biological drives.
Since he *must* have air, water, food, and sex to sur-
vive, his thought, no matter how remote it may *seem*
to be from such humble origins, is nonetheless basically, directly or indirectly, oriented toward the satisfaction of these simple animal wants. One might
have been justifiably suspicious of such a biological
mismatch between a high powered informational capability and a low powered motivational capability on
a priori grounds. The empirical evidence against such a
conception of motivation has existed for a long time
—but it has been taken seriously only recently. As
the drive conception began to be questioned more and
more new evidence against it began to accumulate.
First came the accidental and revolutionary discovery
of the "joy" and aversive centers in the brain. When
these were electrically stimulated, animals would exert
themselves strenuously and continuously in order to
keep being stimulated in the joy centers or to turn the
stimulation off in the aversive centers. The motivating
power of such stimulation was relatively independent
of the state of drive satisfaction or dissatisfaction.
Next there appeared more and more evidence that
animals could be "interested" in novelty per se, that
they would work to solve problems just because they
were new and appeared to arouse the animals' "curiosity." If monkeys, and even rats, could be attracted
by novelty and would exert themselves to solve problems because their curiosity had been aroused, whether
or not there was any food or water payoff, then
surely the nature of man's curiosity had to be re-
examined. It now appears that there are primary *biological* motives *other* than the drives of hunger, thirst,

air, and sex. These are the primary *affects* or feelings
—of surprise, interest, enjoyment, distress, fear, anger,
shame, and contempt. Man is born with these innate
mechanisms which, when activated, produce responses
which are experienced as feelings—which motivate
him toward or away from their apparent source. And
so it becomes possible for one man to learn to feel
interest in mathematics, for another to learn to feel
afraid of mathematics but to be interested in poetry
or in sex—or in anything under the sun but mathematics. In general, then, there is a rough match between the informational possibilities which human
beings can generate and the kinds of motives which
prompt pursuit or avoidance of these diverse possibilities. Human beings can become interested in, or afraid
of, as many things as they can conceive of.

What are the consequences of such a theory for our
understanding of the nature of inner experience and
of daydreaming in particular?

There has been a consensus in the extroverted American ideology that daydreaming is at best a trivial epi-
phenomenon and at its worst a sickness of the spirit
which alienates the individual from nature and society. American psychologists have by and large
shared these prejudices. Introversion has not been the
preferred mode of functioning for the descendants of
the American activist pioneers even when they have
chosen to devote their lives to the study of human
beings. Not only daydreaming but the role of consciousness in general was grossly neglected in the extroverted behavioristic phase now drawing to a close.
Freud had also belittled the significance of consciousness. For him it was the epiphenomenal servant of the
unconscious id. The daydream he conceived to be a

makeshift, compensatory substitute for the real thing —either an imagined nutritive breast or an imagined sexual encounter, or a sublimated, disguised form of such wish-fulfilling drive gratification.

In place of our present conceptions of the daydream as either trivial or pathological or as sublimated drive gratification, Professor Singer has projected a new vista of the daydream as a major human function. Following in the great tradition of Galton and Freud, he has had the courage to use himself as his first, but not last, subject. We now learn from his work that ninety-six per cent of normal Americans report that they engage in some form of daydreaming daily. If daydreaming is a trivial activity, then most Americans are wasting some part of every day. If it is a pathological activity, then most Americans are sick. If it represents a sublimated drive gratification, then most Americans are either underfed, underwatered, or undersexed.

Against the conception of daydreaming as primarily pathological is the recent finding that introverted children are least likely to end up as schizophrenic and that adult schizophrenics are more often hyperactive and antisocial rather than shy and withdrawn in their childhood. Further, hallucinators showed less daydreaming than non-hallucinators, suggesting that daydreaming prepares the adult to accept his own inner processes and to differentiate fantasy from reality more precisely. Daydreaming is, then, neither trivial nor pathological, but emerges as an important human ability which requires practise if it is to be developed and such practise itself requires some degree of privacy. It is not to be confused with "mind wandering" (with which it is indeed negatively correlated) but is a skill available for the enhancement and enrichment of life.

Professor Singer reminds us that the development of the inner life has been excessively derogated both in American psychology and in American culture generally. This problem necessarily implicates the values of the protagonists and it is appropriate that those like Professor Singer who cherish a rich inner life should plead for its importance against the dominant American extroversive ideology. The unexamined life, as Socrates long ago insisted, is not worth living and a life lived without phantasy and daydream may be a seriously impoverished life. There is of course a pluralism of possible good lives. Men may live equally well a life of action or thought or feeling. We are indebted to Professor Singer for illuminating a major mode of experience which the dominant culture has encroached upon and all but submerged.

Silvan S. Tomkins
Center for Research in Cognition and Affect
The City University of New York

Preface

The objective of this book is to re-examine the phenomenon of daydreaming as a psychological problem. In its early days when psychology was considered the science of mental life, investigators paid serious attention to human responses such as imagery, daydreams, and the stream of consciousness. But during the past half century, with Watson's behaviorism and operationalism as the dominant American *Zeitgeist*, there has been relatively little systematic study of spontaneous imagery or conscious fantasy. Only psychoanalysis as a discipline has collected information about patterns of consciousness, dreams, daydreams, and marginal states of awareness.

For all the richness of these clinical reports, however, psychoanalysis, because of its therapeutic emphasis, can provide only anecdotal data or theoretical speculation at levels too removed from operational formulation to meet the highest scientific criteria. Moreover, the orientation within psychoanalysis towards symbolic interpretation of motives expressed in dreams or daydreams, while admittedly a great contribution to our psychological sophistication, has tended somewhat to minimize cognitive and structural dimensions of thought. It is true that with the development of ego psychology in the work of Hartmann, Kris, Erikson, Rapaport, and others, psychoanalytic investigators have shown increased interest in the manifest content of mental products. Yet there remains a serious question whether the psychoanalytic method can ever be more than a hypothesis-engendering agent providing clues and tentative suggestions that still require formal support by controlled experiment and large-scale data-gathering.

The methodological breakthrough in studies of dreaming by electro-physiological means has recently revived interest in mental life. Even if some initial interpretations of their results can be questioned, the work of Dement, Kleitman, and an increasing band of workers has had a healthy impact on the morale of investigators seeking systematic means of studying the inner consciousness of man. My own research, which for the past fifteen years has dealt with the phenomena of daydreaming and conscious fantasy behavior, has given me an increasing awareness of possibilities for better-controlled studies in these fields. By setting down in simple outline some of my own thinking, based upon my observations as a psychoanalyst and clinical psychologist, as a research investigator attempting to obtain ordered information, and as an introspective individual, I hope that I can stimulate a more effective attack on the many research problems having to do with daydreaming and conscious fantasy. I hope also to encourage more disciplined thought about these phenomena by persons whose work is essentially geared toward practical application. My efforts may prove useful if, by raising many questions that seem to need answering, they succeed in engendering a constructive curiosity. Science progresses as much by putting more and more precise questions as by obtaining the right answers. I hope that I can help its advance in psychology by posing some reasonably well-stated queries about the phenomena of daydreaming and fantasy.

The present volume is organized to provide a progressive exploration of the study of fantasy. It begins with a report of personal experience through autobiography and self-experimentation, then examines group data obtained through questionnaire and interview techniques, formal experiments, and developmentally organized findings and theories. Finally, it attempts a tentative statement concerning practical implications of the research on daydreaming for education and psychotherapy. Since one of my aims is to encourage research—by undergraduate or graduate students as well as mature scientists—most sections conclude with some fairly specific suggestions for further experimentation.

This brief volume approaches daydreaming as a fluid, dynamic experience. Certain closely related issues in the broader sphere of the psychology of thinking are not stressed. Imagery is of course the basic stuff of daydreams but the nature of imagery *per se* as a phenomenon requires a separate and more extensive treatment. Regarded as a conscious effort at mental reproduction of actually perceived objects, imagery has been extensively treated most recently in McKellar's *Imagination and Thinking* (1957). Yet there is very little overlap in content between the study of spontaneous cognitive processes reported in the present volume and McKellar's treatment of phenomena such as eidetic imagery or the individual differences in modalities of imagery production. Ultimately, when more extensive empirical research and theoretical sophistication permit, the time may be ripe for a large-scale and detailed examination of the psychology of thought. Such a volume would bring together such topics as imagery, memory, daydreams, hypnagogic and hypnopompic experiences (hallucinatory phenomena prior to and following sleep), night dreams, hallucinations, and the great range of problem-solving controlled thought such as abstraction, concept-formation strategies, and the many "higher mental processes."

I have had considerable help in my investigations —first from friends, relatives, and innocent bystanders who have been the willing or unknowing subjects of my observations, then from patients encountered in almost twenty years as a clinical psychologist, from a host of nameless subjects in a variety of experimental studies, and from a large number of stimulating teachers and valued research collaborators, assistants, and students. My most significant intellectual stimulation has come from the writings in this field of Sigmund Freud, Gardner Murphy, Kurt Lewin, Heinz Werner, Jean Piaget, David Rapaport, Ernst Schachtel, Hermann Rorschach, and Henry Murray, and I have benefited from personal contact with such thinkers as Silvan Tomkins, Francis W. Irwin, Robert Holt, Meyer Maskin, Edward S. Tauber, Sheldon Korchin, Julian Meltzoff, and Harold Basowitz. My experimental research activity has been extensively supported by the Veterans Administration, where Dr. Seymour Klebanoff was especially helpful, and by United States Public Health Service National Institutes of Health Grants M-2279, M-6174, and

MH–08364. My research collaborators have been many, each stimulating and important in his or her own way. Vivian McCraven, Harold Wilensky, Ralph Colvin, George Goldman, Herbert Spohn, Jack Herman, Leone Lesser, Abram Chipman, Phyllis Levy, Claire Fishman, Stanley Feldstein, Marlin Brenner, Aida Kheshishian, Judith Antrobus, Dennis Mourer, and many others have worked closely with me on various specific studies. Laurance Shaffer and Rosalea Schonbar at Teachers College, Columbia University, have been of great assistance in connection with my research there, and Robert L. Thorndike, the late Irving Lorge, and Dorothy Heft have provided me with significant substantive and administrative assistance. I have particularly valued research collaboration and stimulating intellectual exchanges with Richard Rowe.

Most of all I am indebted to my close collaborator, John S. Antrobus, who as a student and as a colleague has shown a loyalty and fierce devotion to clarity and consistency as well as a technical originality that have contributed greatly to every aspect of our research program. Mrs. Helen Glixon has helped considerably in preparation of the manuscript and the index. My wife, Dorothy, has made a significant sacrifice in delaying the flowering of her own promising professional career in order to provide me with the time and psychological freedom to carry on my investigations. The useful comments of a professional and editorial nature provided by L. Joseph Stone of Vassar College and Judith Hillery Higgins of Random House have been most helpful.

Contents

DAYDREAMING

Chapter

I

DAYDREAMING
AS A PSYCHOLOGICAL
PROBLEM

Daydreaming, man's capacity to "give to airy nothing a local habitation and a name," remains one of the most fascinating, if perplexing phenomena of our behavioral repertory. Associated in common language with terms such as "reverie," "brown study," "woolgathering," "castles-in-Spain," daydreaming has been recognized as a fairly widespread human experience. Generally the word is used to mean a shift of attention away from an ongoing physical or mental task or from a perceptual response to external stimulation towards a response to some internal stimulus. The inner processes usually considered are "pictures in the mind's eye," the unrolling of a sequence of events, memories, or creatively constructed images of future events of various degrees of probability of occurrence. Also included as objects of daydreaming are introspective awareness of bodily sensations, affects, or *monologues intérieurs*. While wish fulfillment is a frequent feature of the content of waking fantasy, common usage and the sparse scientific literature have also noted daydreaming's planful or constructive aspects, as well as its anxiety-ridden or obsessional character in particular individuals or at different periods for a given person.

The child who, dawdling at his dinner, is heard softly imitating the sounds of Indian war whoops and pioneers' gunfire is engaged in an early form of daydreaming. The busy executive who finds himself contemplating a forthcoming romantic rendezvous while reading over profit and loss statements, and the harried housewife who while stirring the soup sees herself as a member of royalty at a gala affair, are familiar examples. The absent-minded professor who fumbles with his key at the wrong apartment door as he inwardly contrasts two alternate readings of an ambiguous passage in a medieval manuscript is demonstrating both the distracting nature of daydreaming under certain circumstances and its problem-solving character.

Of course daydreaming or conscious fantasy seems most likely to occur under conditions relatively similar to those of night dreaming. The person alone in a situation of minimal external stimulation, perhaps most often just prior to sleep, is likely to find himself engaged in a reverie or interior monologue. Terms such as James's "stream of consciousness" or Stekel's "polyphony of thought" represent efforts to characterize the complexity of the process of waking awareness with its interplay of direct perceptual response, interpretation of such response, and intrusion of associated phrases or memories, fantasies, fleeting images, and half-heard sounds. An important literary trend of the first third of the present century has been the effort, culminating in Joyce's *Finnegans Wake*, to depict the complex layers of man's ongoing mental activity, conscious and unconscious.

From a psychological viewpoint, the phenomenon of daydreaming poses a number of questions that must be confronted by any theory of personality or any attempt at a sophisticated formulation of a theory of the relationship of neural structure to thinking. The psychology of thought includes such problems as the nature of concept formation, problem-solving strategies, the relationship of abstract to concrete thinking, associational fluidity, and the effects of brain damage on thought and language. An ultimate theory would have to account for daydreaming in relation to these other dimensions of mentation, but here they will be dealt with only in passing.

Before we examine daydreaming as a psychological problem, it is first necessary to comment on what constitutes the scientific approach to the study of such a phenomenon. In psychology we are still at the stage in many aspects of human behavior where we require fairly clear and well-organized descriptions of phenomena before we can move on to a more sophisticated phase of theory construction and experimental test. This is true about daydreaming. We may believe that most people daydream, but closer examination of the evidence leaves us in grave doubt. Much of the work done in questioning people about their inner experiences has been carried out with very small numbers of persons, generally of the better-educated classes, often persons already trained for introspection by the nature of their literary interests or scholarly activity. McKellar (1957) has ably documented many of the differences that people manifest in imagery, but most of his examples are again drawn from well-educated persons. That Coleridge and De Quincey or Virginia Woolf and Joyce had vivid fantasy lives can scarcely be doubted, but that the characters they created would in actuality demonstrate the layers of complex thought assigned them is far less certain.

We need, therefore, to obtain some kinds of information about the true extent of inner mental activity in various samples of our species. To what extent do people generally engage in daydreaming and with what frequency? Can we, indeed, speak of daydreaming as a single phenomenon, or do people differ along a variety of dimensions in their daydreaming patterns?

Other questions which arise include:

1. Can we ascertain whether all persons have a continuous stream of thought to which they attend only when external cues are reduced, as in relaxation, sleep, or the quiet of a psychoanalyst's office? What are the conditions governing the individual's assignment of priorities for attending to external or internal stimuli?

2. Can we formulate any theoretical statement concerning the function of daydreaming in personality organization? So far the major effort in this direction has come from Freud and his followers but their clinically derived hypotheses require experimental demonstration.

We shall later on present some examples of experimental approaches to these questions, which call for fairly sophisticated experimental exploration if we are to move beyond the anecdotal level in theory construction.

Still another general question which calls for both

survey and experimental effort has to do with the development of daydreaming in childhood:

3. Does fantasy play eventually become internalized as daydreaming? Can we specify some of the conditions of a child's experience that foster the development of increased responsiveness to inner stimulation? There has been relatively little formal research dealing with these questions despite many interesting clinical and general observational reports.

The objectives of this brief volume permit only a limited examination of the history of man's effort to study his daydreams and inner stream of thought. It may be desirable to sketch quickly some of the earlier artistic and psychological approaches to fantasy, in the hope of whetting the reader's appetite for more extensive personal examination of some of these sources.

Artistic Approaches to Daydreaming

From the visions of Ezekiel or St. John, which probably represented daydreams cast in literary form for hortatory purposes, to the almost pure fantasy of the recent Theatre of the Absurd or the self-conscious rumination of a Sarraute or Robbe-Grillet, man has expressed his stream of thought in artistic form. The daydreamer as a personality, the daydream as a source of content, and the nature of the thought stream have all been of interest to artists and writers. Socrates is described by Plato as capable of standing all day in the market place lost in thought and oblivious of the external world. Aristophanes' theatrical parody of sophistry caricatured Socrates as seeking to be elevated to the heavens by machine and gave the world the phrase about the impractical daydreamer, "His head is in the clouds." References to daydreaming in Renaissance literature reflect the creative conflict of the period between speculation and action—Cervantes' tragicomic portrayal of Don Quixote, for example, and Shakespeare's depiction of Hamlet decrying his own hesitation by his bitter reference to "John-a-dreams."

The reaction to the overly controlled conscious rationalism of the eighteenth century led to a great revival of Renaissance interest in fantasy during the Romantic period that characterized most of the nineteenth century. The quasi-hallucinatory painting and poetry of Blake, the lush self-consciousness of Goethe's Werther, and the fantastic and daydreamlike stories and prose poems of Hoffmann and Novalis, as well as the poetry and criticism of Coleridge and De Quincey, among others—all reflect a great inward turn of literature. Poe, Hawthorne, and Melville in America, and Baudelaire, Mallarmé, and Flaubert (at least in *Madame Bovary*) in France, also reflect the heightened sensitivity of Romantic writers to ongoing inner stimulation. In music one might mention Schubert and Schumann's song cycles, Berlioz's *Symphonie Fantastique*, and Tchaikovsky's *Symphony No. 1* ("Winter Daydreams") as examples of the innumerable efforts of the composers of that period to portray man's introspective activity in tonal form.

Dostoevski, of course, made moving and psychologically profound use of daydream material in his novels. Robert Louis Stevenson, a minor figure by comparison, was quite sensitive to children's daydreams and wrote an essay on the subject as well as his children's poetry, while Mark Twain was one of the first great writers to capture the fantasy play of children in literary form. It was after the turn of the century, with a somewhat greater interaction between psychology, psychoanalysis, and literature, that the "stream of consciousness" technique reached its flower in the work of Proust, Dorothy Richardson, Virginia Woolf, Joyce, and Faulkner. The significance of this development is brought out in Humphrey's *Stream of Consciousness in the Modern Novel* (1958). Although Hemingway's influence focused attention on "clean," unself-conscious writing with emphasis on direct perception, even in the first-person style, strong literary and dramatic uses of daydreamlike techniques are still evident in the plays of O'Neill and Williams and in the novels of Bellow, or in the film, "The Pawnbroker."

There seems little question that literature and to a much lesser extent art and music have drawn heavily upon sensitivity to inner fantasies, the awareness of an ongoing internal thought stream, and the dry voice of the *monologue intérieur*. Indeed, a definitive study of the subtle relationships between man's daydreaming tendencies as understood psychologically and the use of this tendency for artistic purposes remains to be done, despite significant beginnings by Humphrey (1958) and Hoffman (1959).

A Brief Survey of Psychological Research in Daydreaming

Formal psychological study of fantasy processes has taken two general lines. One has employed various ambiguous or loosely structured stimulus materials to elicit fantasy. This approach, closely associated with the development of the projective techniques in clinical diagnosis and personality research, has led to a voluminous literature and significant advances in psychological understanding and practice. However, since fantasy elicited through response to inkblots or ambiguous pictures can tell us little about man's ongoing spontaneous cognitive processes and naturally occurring daydreams, we shall deal only in passing with the data from research with projective techniques like the Rorschach blots and the Thematic Apperception Test.

A second approach, the more direct study of children's or adults' spontaneous fantasies, daydreams, or thought streams, has a surprisingly sparse investigative history. Following the pioneering efforts of Galton (1883) to study individual differences in imagery in the *Inquiries into the Human Faculty*, there was some development of an interest, particularly in Britain and later in Germany under the Jaensch brothers, in studying the process of imagery for its own sake (McKellar, 1957). The first great formal presentation of man's ongoing inner cognitive activity came in William James's chapter on "The Stream of Thought" in his *Principles of Psychology* of 1890. James's interest was chiefly in the more general aspects of the stream of consciousness, although he was for his time unusually sensitive to the relation of the thought stream to a sense of self and to the continuity of normal and abnormal imaginal experience.

Despite considerable controversy and experimental research at the turn of the century on the nature of imagery and its relation to thought, little attention was paid to daydreaming by psychologists except for those whose work with children forced the issue upon them. Early systematic observations of children's imaginative play were carried out by Hall (1891, 1907) and his students and by Vostrovsky (1894) and Smith (1904). Green (1922, 1923) recorded spontaneous daydreams of children he observed over long periods in the classroom and wrote one of the first books on daydreaming that related it to the psychoanalytic knowledge of the period. He emphasized fantasy content rather more than structure of daydreams. Others who carried out careful observations of children's play as a clue to ongoing inner daydreams included Sherman (1934), Griffiths (1935), Markey (1935), Isaacs (1933). The imaginary playmate as one manifestation of the daydream life of children was studied by Hurlock and Burstein (1932), Jersild, Markey, and Jersild (1933), and Ames and Learned (1946). Murphy, Murphy, and Newcomb (1937) showed an early sensitivity to the constructive as well as defensive features of fantasy play in children. Both Murphy (1947) and Jersild (1960), as early pioneers in the study of a fantasy process as an integral feature of child development, have foreshadowed much current thinking in psychology and psychoanalysis about the adaptive aspects of daydreaming and its relation to the development of what White (1959) has termed the concept of "competence."

In 1907 and 1908 Sigmund Freud showed a particular interest in daydreams and produced several seminal papers (Freud, 1962, Volume IX) which attempted to explore the wish-fulfilling function of daydreams and their relation to the onset of hysterical symptoms. His treatment, albeit brief, is remarkably comprehensive in scope. Nevertheless, despite the central role which daydreams or unconscious fantasies play in Freud's theory of thought as well as his clinical formulations, he included in his writing surprisingly little empirical study of the daydreams of normal individuals. Introspective accounts of personal daydreams were reported by Varendonck (1921) with an introduction by Freud, and Silberer carried out some ingenious self-experiments (elaborated on in Chapter 3) to study the symbolism of hypnagogic imagery (Rapaport, 1951). Shaffer (1936), working outside the psychoanalytic tradition but cognizant of its import, was one of the first psychologists to attempt a direct inquiry into the content of daydreams of normal adults. He used a questionnaire with categories such as "heroic achievement" and by this method was able to study patterns of daydreams over three generations. Seeman (1951), following up Shaffer's work, sought to relate it more directly to Freud's theory of wish fulfillment and found support for the notion that most daydreams do represent wishes in normal adults. More recently, Page (1957) developed a daydream-frequency questionnaire and has carried out some interesting studies on the relationship of Rorschach inkblot factors to daydream frequency and to the content of daydreams and Thematic Apperception Test stories (Page, 1956). Some examples of related questionnaire investigations of daydream frequency will be described in Chapter 3.

Another name which must be mentioned in discussing systematic approaches to daydreaming is that of Henry Murray. Murray's interest in the fantasy response as a clue to motivational patterns and his inspiration of numerous students to devising schemes for scoring and eliciting fantasies are well documented in *Explorations in Personality* (1938). His own development with Morgan of the Thematic Apperception Technique and the great proliferation of research with that ingenious technique has led his students and fol-lowers—for example, Tomkins, Holt, McClelland, Stein, and numerous others—to intensive examination of the art of studying personality through stimulated fantasy. While the great clinical and research utility of the TAT and similar techniques has been brilliantly explored by Murray, McClelland, and the others cited, it is only relatively recently that some like Tomkins and Holt have turned more directly to examination of the spontaneous daydream activities of normal adults.

In summary, the daydream has attracted the interest of a number of persons in psychology who have per-ceived its implications for personality theory. Never-theless, despite brilliant individual comments or brief empirical studies, no consistent series nor any research program dealing with the phenomena of daydreaming emerge from an examination of the literature. When one considers the number of books and empirical stud-ies on nocturnal dreaming the neglect of research on daydreaming seems all the more remarkable. The widespread nature of the phenomenon, its daily occur-rence in our lives, has perhaps caused it to be over-looked (except by writers) as too commonplace for scientific inquiry. But because it is so much a part of our lives, daydreaming merits study. Its existence as a phenomenon raises important problems for the study of human attention processes, the sources of effective stimulation, the motivational or defensive character of fantasy, and many similar issues that must be explained in any theory of human behavior or the physiology of the central nervous system.

Chapter

2

INTROSPECTIVE STUDIES OF FANTASY: OBSERVATION AND EXPERIMENT ON A SAMPLE OF ONE

Let us begin our exploration of the world of day-dreams at their source—the consciousness of a single individual. Starting with an anecdotal account of my personal experiences with daydreaming, I shall move to a more detailed examination of introspection—the stream of thought as I have observed it in myself. I shall proceed next to a presentation of more formal, quasi-experimental studies on thought intrusions and on transitional stages of consciousness, also carried out on myself. In doing so, it is my sincere hope that I can encourage others to consider seriously more intensive self-examination and self-experimentation as an explicit starting point for psychological research.

Some Personal Daydream Experiences

Man's curiosity about daydreams stems not only from accounts of others but from a frequent awareness of the recurrence of these phenomena in his own daily life. In opening with an account of personal experience, I am motivated not only by narcissism but by a conviction that most psychological research ought properly to begin at this point. Too often psychologists carry on a line of investigation which derives from an observed flaw in the experimental design of someone else's research. A chain of studies may grow from such attempts to modify a particular experiment or psychological test, yet the value of the original hypothesis or its significance in man's life may be relatively trivial. While introspection cannot be used to make conclusive statements about phenomena or to test hypotheses, it can serve to sharpen the psychologist's critical awareness of the *relevance* of the experimental material. Such self-examination can also raise legitimate questions for more systematic study. I believe there is nothing essentially wrong in a psychologist's "seeking to solve his own problems through his theory or research," provided that he scrupulously exposes his self-derived data to the rigors of scientific formulation and experimental verification. Indeed, I believe that if more psychologists were themselves willing to undergo the tests they devise or the experimental procedures to which they subject others, we would find a marked upsurge in the significance and vitality of research.

An account of my personal daydream history is therefore provided as a suggested starting point for an extensive investigation. Short of an autobiography, it seems impractical to attempt to present an intensive exploration of the origins and implications of one's fantasies. Selection is necessarily involved in this description of my own daydreaming pattern. The choice of content reflects an effort to explore some relevant dimensions of spontaneous fantasy. However idiosyncratic these experiences may appear to some readers, most of the phenomena have also been reported by other persons, sane and insane. Let me urge the hastily interpreting reader to take a fresh look at his own stream of thought and daydreams before casting the first diagnostic label!

The types of daydreaming which I have observed in myself fall fairly readily into two categories. There are a number of repeated, self-consistent, and elaborate fantasies which have persisted for years since childhood and which have an almost independent existence. They have recurred frequently, sometimes spontaneously, and have more often than not been consciously engaged in under specific circumstances. A second category includes the greater bulk of my reverie activity over the years—the ongoing stream of associations, interior monologues, and occasional elaborated fantasies of a spontaneous nature associated with particular problems or chains of thought.

RECURRENT DAYDREAMS

An important feature of my mental life in childhood and adolescence was my interest in a series of recurring fantasies. Most of these (they numbered as many as a dozen in early adolescence) involved the adventures of a heroic figure, generally a person of outstanding character and achievement in a specific field of endeavor. I generally made a clear separation between myself and the characters, with one exception, and usually allowed them to run an independent life course, or particular phase of their adventures. The closest literary approximation of this pattern may be found in the famous Walter Mitty story by James Thurber. We cannot tell from Thurber's story whether the heroic figures who enter Mitty's consciousness are recurrent. While in my own case over the years I have had hundreds of fleeting fantasies of heroic achievements or attainment of specific goals that resemble Mitty's, the main emphasis in my daydreams has been on a recurrent group of characters.

The fantasies grew out of my pattern of childhood play activity supplemented by reading or movie-going during ages seven to eleven. At first the characters were part of private play, an activity engaged in alone with elaborate physical activity, talking aloud, and active role-playing of various ancillary characters. Some of these characters were also initially included in play with other children. When elaborate fantasy play diminished, giving way more to organized formal games or sports, these figures persisted in private play or in drawing. As school and social play came to make increasing demands upon my time, and as I became aware of the social embarrassment of continued overt fantasy, my indulgence of these fantasy characters took the form of drawing. Later they became almost wholly internalized in visual imagery.

The drawings generally consisted of particular sequences of adventures sketched like comic strips except that, since the fantasy was played out internally, captions were unnecessary. My drawing skill was applied to delineating the main characters of a fantasy, but the emphasis was almost always on the story rather than the drawing. I became fairly skillful at suggesting activity with a few rapid strokes but this skill was almost completely in the service of the fantasy play and had relatively little subsequent social utility in school art courses or in winning approval from others. The drawings undoubtedly played a part in feeding back a more crystallized visual image of the characters involved in the fantasies. These visual images were made yet more vivid by my linking them to particularly appealing personalities whom I saw in movies or occasionally met in real life.

By far the most personally interesting of my daydream activity in puberty and adolescence centered on the recurring "central figure" fantasies. The following examples represent some forms which these fantasies took and are presented in detail because of their typicality, their persistence into adult life, and the degree to which I have been able to trace their development and relationship to my own general personality. A comparable exploration of their own fantasies might prove an instructive exercise for interested readers.

Poppy Ott Fantasy—Football Hero. At about the age of nine I began reading a series of boy's books describing the adventures of a group of friends living in a mythical small Midwestern town, Tutter. In reading each book of the extensive series, I gradually became particularly fond of one of the characters, Poppy Ott, who seemed clever and intellectually gifted. My interest in these books waned after a few years, but my liking for the character of Poppy Ott persisted. I had in the meantime developed a considerable interest in sports and began to engage in elaborate fantasied football games. Initially these took the form of actual running and jumping and simulating in detail the events of a full game in which I tackled myself, caught my own passes, and generally enjoyed an active motor participation. Soon I found myself making up my own league and using the characters and locales from the Tutter books, although the original series itself had nothing to do with football. Within the format of fantasied football games, Poppy Ott emerged as the super-star, the shifty-hipped, clever broken-field runner and accurate passer. As time passed the overt motor representation of an imagined game was no longer socially feasible and I began to draw the game on paper in cartoon form. I would visualize an entire league series, draw significant highlights from each game, occasionally write out play-by-play accounts of the games, and keep statistics on the various achievements of my fantasy players in the same way that the newspapers do for running or passing averages.

As I grew into adolescence, Poppy Ott, who was supposedly a few years older than I was, grew up too. He left Tutter to play professional football and, after some well-documented setbacks, emerged as the greatest football player of all time on a Boston professional team of my own creation. Eventually less of this material was written down or drawn and more was visualized. The fantasy was closely correlated with the actual football season; during the spring and summer it was shelved for a comparably elaborate baseball fantasy with a different cast of characters.

Finally, the entire fantasy sequence settled into a fairly circumscribed pattern. In high school and even into adult life I would deal with situations that were monotonous or dull by resorting consciously to playing out a particular game in which Poppy Ott starred. At classes in school I might doodle cartoons depicting events of a fantasied game, or in a variety of military situations that involved long waiting or a solitary vigil I would amuse myself by fantasizing games. Although many other demands have pre-empted my consciousness, the fantasy continues to be available and on occasion still helps me to while away a long train ride when I do not feel up to more "constructive" thinking. It has also recurred in situations such as long nights' vigils with sick babies or has permitted me to tune out rock and roll music in situations where I have been a captive audience. The use of the fantasy chiefly to deal with a dull external situation emerged only gradually, however. In childhood and early adolescence I eagerly looked forward to an occasion when I could be alone to think about Poppy Ott.

"Great Statesman" Fantasy. Another central figure heroic fantasy which developed about the same time as the football or baseball fantasies contrasted markedly with them in content but not in underlying dynamic characteristics. Perhaps as an outgrowth of my early political awareness and an active role in elementary school debates, an imaginary figure of a great senator began to occur in my daydreams. Beginning as a crusading, reform district attorney who fought the corrupt political bosses and racketeers, this man eventually rose to be a dynamic and distinguished senator. Just as my football hero was the greatest of all time and my baseball heroes rivalled Ty Cobb and Babe Ruth, the senator emerged in recurrent daydreams as a towering national leader. In fantasied incident after incident he shone forth as the great moral figure of

American life, a foe of corruption or blind conservatism, the bulwark of the republic, a towering intellect in the service of his people. The cliché language of the last sentence, reminiscent of political campaign oratory, nevertheless describes the accomplishments of my senator as he appeared in my mind's eye. Exposure of private fantasies is painful not only because it reveals inner dynamic trends, ordinarily concealed, but also because it exposes the soap opera, cliché-ridden quality of much thought. The senator fantasy did not seen banal to me, however, at ages eleven to eighteen.

The earliest phase of the senator theme (I never settled on a name for him) was acted out physically in my play. Later this fantasy was transferred to drawings of the cartoon type and eventually was limited only to mental representation. In drawings the senator and some of his antagonists took on distinct physical appearances and even now, although the daydream scarcely recurs, I can still draw the face of the senator. He appeared as a distinguished, white-haired, Van-dyke-bearded gentleman, rather resembling Senator Henry Cabot Lodge in physiognomy but scarcely in political orientation. The senator undoubtedly represented a somewhat modernized version of my own grandfather, whom I had known until his death when I was seven or eight and who had been a legendary family idol.

This daydream soon disappeared almost completely in the press of postwar real life, but the content and specific incidents or the appearance of certain characters are still available to me at will. Unlike the football fantasy, the senator theme (perhaps because it re-

quired more creative effort) never became sufficiently automatic to serve as a time-passing game in
adult life.

"Singer the Great Composer" Fantasy. The third
example of a frequently recurring fantasy also involves a central heroic figure but differs from the
other fantasies because it represented more clearly a
wish on my part and my own name was assigned to
the central character. The mixture of self- and non-
self-identification in this fantasy is curious because,
despite my own expressed love for music and wish
that I might really be a composer, I never thought of
the fantasy in the first person.

Initially this fantasy grew out of my crude attempts at playing the piano when I was about ten.
Although I had had no instruction, I gradually learned
to play by ear and while I lacked any technical skill I
was adroit at making up original melodies. As I sat
more or less banging away, I began substituting inner
harmony for the rather mediocre external stimuli I
was creating. I began imagining operas, symphonies,
and a variety of musical works. Gradually the character of Singer the composer emerged as well as a host
of associated characters, entirely fictional, with appropriate Italian names, who were the soloists in the
operas.

As my technique improved somewhat and as I read
more about music, I began keeping notebooks docu-
menting the various works of Singer from his first
success (a five-act grand opera setting of Longfellow's
Evangeline, which my English class studied in seventh or eighth grade) to his mature chamber works
and great symphonies. I wrote out detailed accounts of
the action and musical quality of various operas and

played them through at length, undoubtedly with great variation except for the themes and main structural lines of development. Singer grew older as his works proliferated and eventually he was a very old man, still working on his *Seventh Symphony*, which, like Sibelius' *Eighth*, it appears he will not finish, unless I find myself reverting to this fantasy in *my* old age.

Gradually I spent less time in the fantasy play at the piano or in writing the notebook descriptions of the music. Singer lived on in imagery form, however, and would recur at times in later adolescence when I improvised at a piano (the music would be a work of *his*). Often when alone I drifted into a musical daydream, perhaps imitating the sounds of an orchestra and running through a section of one or another of Singer's works. This fantasy activity has never really ceased, and in idle moments I still have musical daydreams which take the form of audibly or inaudibly humming or singing excerpts from Singer's works or from some of the rival composers whom I also created. On the whole, however, the fantasy has faded to a pale shadow of the richness and excitement it had for me in early adolescence. Like the Poppy Ott football fantasy, the Singer music fantasy has become crystallized into a relatively narrow form for use in idle moments, in this case the internal playing out of a symphony replacing the football game sequence.

Some Implications of These Recurrent Fantasies. Let me briefly summarize some of the main implications of the observations I have made on the basis of my recurrent daydreams. It should be obvious that the pattern manifests a high degree of general achievement motivation, a striving which quite obviously characterized my overt behavior as well as my fantasy. At the same time, a subtle relationship emerges between specific content and actual accomplishment since I never became a senator, composer, or football star. Some reality is involved in each fantasy, however, because I became somewhat involved in school or professional-society politics, I did play sandlot football with moderate success, and did indeed eventually write a little music.

The composer fantasy, closest of all to a conscious wish, exemplifies an important principle which is supported by clinical observation. My actual musical efforts proved so inferior to my fantasy that I quickly abandoned efforts to learn music properly. Indeed, clinical observation of patients blocked in writing or creative work has often suggested that a grandiose fantasy standard makes every effort seem hopelessly inferior so that the effort of narrowing this gap appears too heavy a burden. An experimental approach to this notion might well involve a level of aspiration technique and an analysis of the high-goal subjects' evasions.

What of the emotions accompanying these fantasies?

The most general affective concomitants of these longstanding daydreams have been a moderate degree of pleasure and excitement. Occasionally some specific fantasy might also be associated with sexual arousal or excitement. Relatively early, however, the fantasies that were particularly conducive to strong sexual arousal took on a fairly definite form and were limited to very specific content patterns with almost no overlap. On the whole, while a fantasy experience was rarely as exciting or joyous as the excitement of an actual success—for example, in a real football game—I did experience considerable positive feeling in the course of the daydreams.

My daydreams were rarely accompanied by unpleasant feelings. Perhaps the most common negative affect associated with my fantasy life was shame. This affect seemed closely related to the socialization process. The shame occurred when I contemplated being discovered in the act of play or talking aloud to myself. I also felt embarrassed lest others discover the degree to which my fantasies were grandiose and unrealistic. I now realize that my family was more than usually tolerant of overt fantasy play so that I was permitted to carry it on with a minimum of interruption or teasing. I quickly learned that such acceptance at home was scarcely mirrored by the outside world, and this no doubt played a part in the development of my shame and secrecy concerning fantasy. Certainly the internalization and often enough the relative disappearance of daydreaming in many people is closely linked to its association with childishness. The circumstances in my own life made it possible for me to continue my pleasurable investment in my own daydreams but it became clear that considerable circumspection was necessary to keep them private. When the awareness of the embarrassing significance of this holdover of childhood forced its complete internalization, I had already developed a host of well-crystallized, recurrent *structures*. In effect, fantasy had become a kind of generalized reinforcer, in Skinner's sense, which may not be the case for persons who have been forced to suppress it much earlier in life.

In addition to the obvious achievement motivation,

narcissism, and theme of great success (not at all in the financial or material sense, interestingly), a persisting element in all my fantasies was the need for creative expression and organization. Every fantasy was perforce turned into a story.

Storytelling requires originality (hopefully) and organization. The tendency towards imposing some logical structure on fantasy material suggests that from an early age the operation of what Freud has called secondary process thinking was clearly evident in my fantasy behavior and, incidentally, in my dreams, since these very often took the form of an organized narrative. Holt (1960) has recently provided an analysis of the development of secondary processes which emphasizes their early significance in personality development. Certainly my own introspection accords with this view.

The storytelling aspect of my fantasies also involved some significant hinging of the material to reality. For one thing, the subjects of these fantasies, even in the case of Singer the composer, were not identical with myself. Secondly, the heroic activities of the characters were within the realm of reasonable possibility. The Superman or Batman fantasies of comic books, in which the activities are clearly beyond normal capacity (for example, flying, invisibility, X-ray vision), were always somewhat repugnant to me; there was no magic in the successful behavior of my daydream heroes. Finally, the imposition of a sequential logic and a certain rounding out of the material (a characteristic even of my night dreams) clearly represented a form of secondary process operation on the content of my daydreams.

However vivid the imagery of my daydreams, at no

time do I recall confusing them with reality. The extensiveness of the fantasy dimension in my personal experience, while available as a pleasurable means for dealing with free time or escape from a dull external situation, never took on a hallucinatory quality. Although the type of elaborate private worlds I constructed clearly resembles in detail the complex daydream universe created by the young patient in *The Jet-Propelled Couch* (Lindner, 1955), the option of immersing myself in fantasy to the exclusion of the real world, as he did, never seemed available to me even in times of severe emotional distress. Thus, the occurrence of so extensive a fantasy life need not preclude, and in some instances may enhance, the establishment of a clear distinction between reality and fantasy. Moreover, the constant exploration of one's daydream world makes it a familiar realm, less likely to evoke anxiety. It remains a distinct possibility, worthy of more thorough research exploration, that many persons who have failed to indulge in fantasy play may misinterpret vivid daydreams or images as hallucinations and may be made far more anxious by the sudden, seemingly autonomous occurrence of a fantasy image or phrase of a conversation.

In general, my own personal experience strongly suggests that a fantasy does indeed bear a direct relation to its expression in overt behavior. This would contradict what is often assumed in catharsis theories or in certain approaches to projective-test interpretation: namely, that fantasying about something precludes carrying it out in actual behavior. At any rate, the relationship between fantasy and overt behavior is clearly complex, as was suggested in the brief discussion of the discrepancy between a rigidly held, high-aspiring fantasy and the ineffectual-appearing initial attempts at its fulfillment. In my own case the occurrence of a fairly extensive variety of elaborate and obviously unrealizable daydreams has been associated with at least some small degree of actual overt behavior or achievement in each of these areas. Recently Symonds and Jensen (1961), in a long-term follow-up of persons whose adolescent fantasies they studied, reached a somewhat similar conclusion.

The Stream of Thought and Spontaneous Cognitive Processes

Recurrent, elaborated daydreams of the type just described, however intriguing as a phenomenon, represent an extreme instance and only a fraction of the total amount of ongoing internal cognitive activity. As long as I can remember I have also been aware of an ongoing stream of thought, pervasive and almost uninterrupted, that seems best described by James's concept of the stream of thought and by interior monologue literature. These ongoing associations of mine are often merely slight cognitive or affective footnotes to external perceptions such as a thrill of excitement at the sight of heavy black clouds over a turbulent sea or a curiosity about a lone distant light. Very frequently, however, the stream of thought has been much more of an interpretation or inward comment on perceptions. This comment has taken the form either of an associative image or of a remark by an inner voice (the interior monologue). The former experience is best described in literature by Proust's famous example of the Madeleine crumb which revives by its taste a sudden flood of memories unfolding like Japanese paper flowers in a bowl of water.

The interior monologue has its finest literary expression in the various monologues Joyce assigns to Stephen Dedalus. It is a kind of dry inner voice annotating my external stimulus world or annotating such inner experience as my associative images or various somatic responses (stomach gurglings, for instance). I have been aware of this type of internal running commentary in myself for years. It is by no means as frequent or pervasive as associative imagery, and my impression is that this inner voice does not have so early an origin psychologically as the other aspects of the stream of thought, being to a much larger extent a reflection of literary experience, conventions of first-person singular writing, and a sense of identification with particular characters of fiction. Inquiry of others and clinical observations have suggested that first-person narratives such as the familiar private-eye monologues on radio and television often become incorporated into persons' self-conscious awareness of their responses.

My own experience leads me to the hypothesis that for myself, at any rate, the interior *verbal* monologue was more closely connected with defensive behavior. As a shy adolescent feeling awkward and clumsy at a dance I might stand against a wall and portray myself to myself as the inscrutable observer, the objective commentator on the world's foibles. Masking shyness with an omniscient detachment, my interior monologue would race along with witty and penetrating insights on the characters of the pretty girls with whom I really was dying to dance or the obviously mindless young fellows who actually embraced them.

More recently, serving as a preliminary subject in an experiment we were conducting on electrophysiological concomitants of daydreaming, I was struck by the vivid "loudness" with which my interior monologue began running on. It seemed clear to me that the strangeness of the room, the knowledge that I was wired up, and the curosity and interest I had about the experiment had very likely fostered an upsurge of the detached, self-conscious reportage effect. In a while this inner monologue subsided somewhat but it seemed to run often enough almost concurrently with imagery and visual daydreaming.

CLASSIFICATION OF THE DIMENSIONS OF THE THOUGHT STREAM

Perhaps one way to convey the quality of the stream of internally produced cognitive processes, as I have observed them in myself, is to use a simple conceptualization based on a dimension of stimulus location and intensity. Under waking conditions with eyes open, a vivid external stimulus absorbs all attention and involves minimal inner *conscious* interpretation or association. An explosion, a sudden flash of light, a vividly colored landscape, a new face—all make so strong a demand that little interior activity can be detected. Similarly, active motor responses such as shifting gears, diving into a pool, hitting a tennis ball, laughing or shouting with excitement, seem to preclude much inner cognitive activity. Of course absorption in one's own inner processes can preclude observation of external stimuli but this is less likely. In one instance, however, a patient of mine talked on and on about himself, disregarding my own restlessness and the loud bells and sirens just outside the window which made it all too clear that the building was on fire.

Although not located in the "outside world," insistent bodily sensations, pains, cramps, digestive rumblings, urges to urinate or defecate, or sexual arousal, function in much the same way as more readily observable stimuli and demand attention with only a minimum of inner cognitive activity. Attention to stimuli that are part of what one might call the "running machinery" of sense organs comes next; for example, stomach gurglings, rushings in the ears, spots in front of one's eyes, after-images and phosphenes, and those myriad flickering kaleidoscopic forms that often appear on closing one's eyes. Self-absorbed behavior such as that of chronic schizophrenics or hypochondriacs, which is interpreted by observers as "immersion in a private world of daydreams," frequently turns out on examination to be an extreme preoccupation with bodily sensations, with kinesthetic awareness, or with the play of lights in blurring vision.

Under conditions of fatigue or drowsiness with eyes open, when visual accommodation weakens, I have experienced what can be termed "blank periods." These represent situations when I can in retrospect realize that for a period of time I have been gazing in an unfocused fashion at blurred lights which took no definite form, were assigned no meaning, produced no associations, and evoked no interior comment or even curiosity. These periods seem most like genuine breaks in the stream of consciousness and are probably much like the experience of severely anxious persons, chronic, so-called "burnt-out" mental patients, or patients with severe brain damage.

Moving "inward" along the stimulus dimension one

might next refer to visual or auditory sensations (generally the former) evoked by perceptual responses that are only moderately intense or that have already been somewhat assimilated. The sound of feet running in the next room may lead to an interpretative visual image of the child who is running. A silvery flash against the blue sky may not be fully perceived but almost instantly leads to an associative image of what the image represented, a jet airliner.

External situations may thus touch off a range of associative images from the merely identifying flash of thought, "It's like a plane I flew in," to some interior monologue such as, "There I go again—preoccupied with getting away from it all instead of facing reality," or, at the extreme, into an elaborated visual daydream in which one recalls in detail an actual event or engages in an extended imaginative construction of what an ideal vacation may be. The last-named instance might end up in an extended series of further responses and perhaps associated affective reactions to what are now a variety of internally produced stimuli, with only minimal attention to the external stimulus situation.

Any associate train which by its feedback of memory or fantasy imagery may become a fairly prolonged immersion in daydreaming may also be evoked by awareness of a bodily reaction or by some form of affective experience. The affect itself might have been aroused by an external situation. For example, a sudden loud noise may evoke a startle pattern and, as it subsides, some interest or curiosity (Tomkins, 1962). Failing any clear external stimulus which can absorb one's interest (if, for example, the crash was from a distance and its cause is not detectable perceptually), a chain of daydreaming may be evoked about the causes of the crash, or about one's affective reaction, and this may in turn elicit a series of images or partial reconstructions of similar situations in which this feeling occurred. In psychotherapy one often deals with the extensive reactions persons have to a state of affective arousal which evokes a chain of speculation or recrimination that may lead to even further persisting arousal and despair. The initial affective state need not have been negative but for some persons an awareness of excitement which cannot readily be labeled may itself prove threatening and lead to an extended frightening daydream. Schachter and Singer (1962) have, for example, recently studied the difficulties some individuals have in labeling the sudden states of arousal created by experimental induction of adrenal activity.

As suggested above, then, the daydream represents a form of stimulation which competes with a variety of attention demands upon the individual. It seems clear that it is generally a weaker stimulus and can emerge chiefly under conditions in which external stimuli are greatly reduced, as at bedtime, or under monotonous external conditions, such as traveling an overfamiliar route, while shaving, or performing routine industrial tasks. In my own case—and it is clear from normative studies, in many other persons'—daydreaming and, more generally, thinking, are highly valued and personal activities and are likely to emerge as soon as external demands are even moderately reduced. Once attended to, however, the ongoing stream of thought generates new responses or affective experience and plays a significant role in steering behavior.

To the skilled and habitual introspectionist, nothing in the way of human thought may seem alien, but to the person inexperienced in self-awareness, a vivid image, a perverse sexual idea, or a death wish may seem like a bolt from the blue, so unacceptable that it is often attributed to someone else and regarded as a hallucination. One might hypothesize that a person less familiar with the variegated combinations and fluid associations of his ongoing thought stream might be more suggestible under various quasi-hypnotic situations or under "brain-washing" conditions.

A remarkable exemplification of the description of the stream of thought as a function of source of stimulation and intensity may be found in Humphrey's brilliant *Stream of Consciousness in the Modern Novel.* Humphrey's analysis of Molly Bloom's famous monologue in Joyce's *Ulysses* clearly indicates Joyce's sensitivity to this relation of consciousness to external stimulation. At first, aroused by her husband's late return, Molly stirs restlessly and responds to many external stimuli—the clock, the wallpaper, the lamp. Gradually she is immersed more and more in internally stimulated fantasy, until amidst warm thoughts of her romantic courtship by Leopold Bloom "beneath the Moorish wall" in Gibraltar, she drifts again into sleep.

In summary, then, self-observation suggests that the degree of awareness of a stream of thought is a function of the intensity of external or internal kinesthetic stimulation. Gross physical activity or a rapidly changing or vivid external stimulus field inhibits sensitivity to inner process, while relatively monotonous external conditions increase self-awareness of internal cognitive activity. At the same time the emergent awareness of one's own spontaneous inner activity produces a feedback effect which can generate a new pattern of action, affect, or fantasy. What we do not know, however, is the degree to which such awareness is a function of an individual's cognitive style or is characteristic of all adult thought. I shall return to this problem in discussing experimental studies of the production and suppression of ongoing thought in a later chapter.

SOME SUGGESTIONS FOR FURTHER RESEARCH THROUGH SELF-OBSERVATION

Before turning to a discussion of more systematic quasi-experimental studies carried out on myself, let me briefly note some specific research possibilities suggested by the elaborate introspective activity I have so briefly described here. I should like to propose a more extensive integration of the so-called nomothetic and ideographic approaches to personality study. One might begin by an intensive interview of a small number of individuals concerning their daydreaming and night-dreaming styles and systematically formulate a pattern, if one is discernible, for each. Such patterning might then be used to make predictions of future behavior for each individual or to construct hypotheses for studying contrasted groups. Some questions we might ask include the following:

1. To what extent can we continue to make a distinction between primary and secondary process elements in fantasy; do secondary (for example, structural and logical elements) processes enter very early into daydreaming as reported by adults or adolescents?

2. Can it be demonstrated that some individuals are generally more responsive to ongoing fantasy than others, or will it turn out that when urged almost

anyone can markedly increase awareness of fantasies, marginal thoughts, and night dreams?

3. To what extent, either for individuals or more generally in the population, can daydreaming be shown to function as a stimulating environment—that is, arousing interest and positive affects or engendering new motivation—in contrast to the more general psychoanalytic view that it partially reduces drives?

4. Can we show any systematic pattern of relationship between the style and content of longstanding daydreams and the fantasy patterns emerging on projective tests or the actual behavioral style of the individual? We might examine the relationship, for example, between achievement motivation as measured by McClelland, through storytelling and thematic apperception techniques, and the repetitive fantasies reported by individuals.

5. Is it possible that some persons show almost no pattern of repetitive consistent daydreaming? What significance would it have if a person reported considerable fleeting fantasy but no clearly identified alterego figures or structure to the daydream pattern?

6. To what extent does the degree of relative realism or possibility of occurrence of the fantasy material play a role in behavioral patterns? An unpublished study by Ross, for example, found evidence that women whose daydreams were highly unrealizable were less effective housekeepers than women whose daydreams were of a more probable type. Similarly, an unpublished study by Machiavello found that persons reporting highly unrealistic daydreams tended to set more unrealistic goals for themselves in a formal level-of-aspiration experiment. The subtleties of the relationship between the daydream as a preparation for

reality and as an avoidance of reality demand more careful study. Methods do seem available to approach this experimentally if we are willing to begin by intensive direct questioning of cooperative persons.

Some Experiments on Intrusions of Thought

Let us move next to some more formal examinations of personal experience and the use of oneself as an experimental subject.

One of the defining characteristics of adult daydreaming employed in this investigation has been as a diversion from the course of an ongoing motor performance or directed thought. Most people interviewed in our investigations or responding to questionnaires reported that their greatest amount of daydreaming occurred before sleep, when in a fatigued state and in a transition to unconsciousness. An interesting possibility, therefore, might be to attempt to study more systematically one's own mental processes just prior to sleep or under conditions of drowsiness, while at the same time attempting to maintain a more complex or formal stream of directed thought. This was the technique employed by Silberer (1951) in his studies of symbol formation, and they seemed worthy of replication and extension.

The first step in this formal study involved a systematic self-scrutiny during periods of relaxed drowsiness while performing a mental task. I would await a period, usually late afternoon following a heavy schedule, and relax on a couch or in an easy chair. Then I would assign myself a specific mental task. This might be something fairly mundane, such as a survey of debts and finances, plans for house repairs, or mapping out a schedule of activities for the next weeks to take care of a variety of routine but burdensome chores. At other times the task might be more complex. I might decide to think through in detail the technical problems, transference and countertransference situation, and possible next steps in connection with a particular patient with whom I was working. At other times I might set myself a chore analogous to Silberer's contrast of two philosophical systems—for example, the comparison of the origins of the ego in the Freudian system with Sullivan's description of the origin of the self-system.

As a means of circumscribing each episode, I set an alarm to ring after five minutes. When the alarm rang, I would hastily review the sequence of events. After several trials I became less self-conscious and found that, once under way, I thought less and less about the fact that an "experiment" was in process. Following the review of sequence, I would quickly classify the patterns of thought under a variety of rubrics that had been arrived at after a number of practice trials.

Eventually I was able to settle upon sixteen content categories for the assigned task. I set up four trials of five minutes each (spread over a period of some months) for each of the categories in a prerandomized sequence. Since there were four trials for each content category it was possible to obtain a reasonable degree of reliability for the evaluation of mean differences.

The assigned mental tasks fell into three dimensions:

1. *Simple–Complex*
2. *Reminiscent–Planful or Theoretical*
3. *Personal–Impersonal*

The *Simple–Complex* dimension was defined by

the degree of intellectual complexity and subtlety of the material. The *Reminiscent–Planful or Theoretical* dimension involved a comparison of past-oriented thought as against future-oriented or more critical evaluative thought. Finally, the *Personal–Impersonal* dimension involved the degree to which the material was specifically self-referent. It proved difficult to establish really clear-cut distinctions for some of these assigned mental tasks, but the final grouping used for this particular self-experiment seemed reasonably satisfactory. Table I presents the sixteen assigned tasks grouped into their three classifications. There were two similar tasks (A and B) in each category, and each was employed twice in a randomized sequence to minimize sequence effects.

Following the five minutes of the assigned mental task, I at once classified my experience along the following dimensions:

1. Number of intrusions of unrelated thought, blank periods, or attention to external stimuli.

2. Degree of visual imagery in interrupting thoughts.

3. Degree of nonvisual imagery in interrupting thoughts.

4. Degree of symbolic content in interruptions.

5. Degree of relative personal–impersonal reference in interrupting thoughts.

6. Degree of apparent strain or effort in maintaining continuity of assigned task.

The execution of such a fairly complex experiment with oneself as subject proved difficult, if engrossing. It seems impossible, of course, to avoid biases and great self-consciousness, which necessarily alter results from what they might be if there were no awareness of an ongoing experiment. Certain general trends

TABLE I *Assigned Mental Tasks Grouped into Categories*

| | Simple | | | | Complex | | | |
| | Impersonal | | Personal | | Impersonal | | Personal | |
	Reminis.	Planful	Reminis.	Planful	Reminis.	Planful	Reminis.	Planful
TASK A	Famous dates in American history from 1619 on	Organize a schedule of games for a league of 8 teams	Recall details of life during past 2 summers	Plan schedule of chores and professional activity for coming 2 weeks	Review in sequence actual events of World War II from Sept. 1939 to end of war	Future of university program with 2 alternative approaches to curriculum	Review and analyze the sequence of events in work with a former patient	Contrast current status of 2 patients; consider self and countertransference phenomena and plan for future
TASK B	Recall scenes from Gilbert and Sullivan operettas or words of songs from musical comedies	Figure out specific steps necessary for the preparation of a musical comedy for Broadway production	Recall activities during winter months	Plan a vacation trip and contrast alternate routes of driving to location	Review the sequence of political campaigns in this country since Roosevelt's death	Compare the implications of Freud's and Sullivan's theories of ego and self-system origin	Review lives of parents and facts of their personalities and influence on self	Imagine own future in 10 years and possible important decisions

emerged fairly clearly from the data, however, and suggest the value of a more extensive consideration of this approach with larger numbers of subjects.

In general, the results of the actual tabulation of the ratings suggested a number of trends. The frequency of intrusive thoughts was by far the greatest for complex, impersonal, and planful or theoretical material. Reminiscing proved to be the easiest task and produced fewest interruptions and the least feeling of strain. The most striking overall trend in the content of the interruptions was the very great tendency for visual imagery to become increasingly prominent and to replace either more abstract thought or interior verbalizations. The visual material consisted chiefly of memories, but occasionally there were fairly elaborate fantasies of scenes that *might* take place or merely the translation of some verbal comment into a lengthy visual scene, occasionally with auditory imagery of the conversations or sounds associated with the visual scene faintly present. Material which appeared to be symbolic—that is, seemed to involve phenomena of an allegorical or metaphorical quality similar to dream symbolism—emerged almost exclusively in response to impersonal, planful or theoretical tasks, both simple and complex, although more frequently with the complex material.

Personal reference in the intrusive thoughts generally predominated for all conditions but was more common when the material of the assigned mental task was already personal in content. Another interaction effect which emerged was the tendency for complex, impersonal material to suffer more frequent interruptions of thought than simple, impersonal material,

while complex and simple personal material did not
differ particularly in the number of interruptions.

The impression I gained from this fairly extensive
personal experiment was that under relaxed, slightly
drowsy conditions, the attempt to sustain a continuous, somewhat orderly sequence of thought is fairly
difficult—as Silberer, too, noted. Personalized visual
imagery tended to intrude upon me periodically. The
shift towards such imagery was more likely to occur
with complex, impersonal material than with simple
material, and in the former case there was also a
greater trend towards symbolic material, as we have
noted.

By far the simplest line of thought to maintain was a
memory sequence. Once initiated, a memory sequence
seemed to run its course almost automatically, while
theoretical thought or future planning constantly
called for volitional effort. The contrast between
planful thought and remembering was somewhat analogous to that of the early phases of learning a motor
skill compared with the relative ease, integration, and
quasi-automatic flow of motor activity once the skill
has been acquired. At the same time it should be noted
that the intrusive material was not at all exclusively
reminiscent in content but often enough was personalized wish fulfillment, fleeting planful imagery, or, occasionally, relatively novel constructions or symbolic
transformations.

The symbolic material, which occurred chiefly in
connection with abstract thought, was the only material that seemed somewhat similar to Silberer's reports
of his hypnagogic experiences. An example of such
allegorical transformations was the occurrence of certain vivid visual images during the attempt to compare

Freud's and Sullivan's theories of the ego and self-system. At one time as I was trying to formulate the psychoanalytic conception of the neutralization of energies or the formation of countercathexes, I suddenly became aware that I had drifted into an elaborate image of a kind of giant mechanical amoeba extending pseudopodia which kept turning back upon their author. At another time I had a clear image of a shy young boy in an awkward, defensive position looking wounded and clinging desperately to a kind of silhouette figure. This image seemed to appear not long after I had been pondering the implications of Sullivan's notion that the self-system grew as a defensive measure against anxiety and that it represented a major obstacle to subsequent personality change.

The more general trend, however, was for the occurrence of memories or fantasies that were not specifically symbolic in content. One cannot avoid the implication of a particular idiosyncratic trend in the emphases of visual imagery intrusions. My long history of visual daydreaming must certainly be taken into account and, in addition, my relatively high interest in people rather than in objects, mechanical operations, or abstract formulations. Generally, symbolism of the condensed or displaced type has played a limited role in my conscious fantasy or even my dreams, and it seems to be again less conspicuous in this formal study.

It seems quite clear that a study of this type must be extended to larger numbers of subjects where general population trends as well as idiosyncratic patterns can be evaluated. Preliminary investigations with students in groups utilizing a somewhat similar design and suitably appropriate content in the assigned tasks have begun, but many of the technical methodological problems remain to be resolved. Initial observation suggests general support for the finding that in relaxed or sleepy states thought shifts from an orderly sequence to visual imagery and for the finding that a reminiscent strain of thought is easier to maintain than a planful or theoretical one. Attempts to employ this method described above with persons on whom electrophysiological measurements of eye movement and electro-encephalogram and electromyographic recordings are obtainable are also under way.

As the methodology of this type of experiment is perfected, it can be used increasingly for study of more formal theoretical issues. Is visual imagery, for example, the most pervasive underlying feature of the ongoing thought stream? The group data I have collected suggest this to be the case—for college students, at any rate—but it is certainly true that in almost every group, I have turned up at least one student who denies visual imagery and thinks others who have it must be peculiar. Are these differences in modality essentially idiosyncratic accidents or do they have broader implications? McKellar (1957) has summarized the current status of the problem of imagery differences, but there is little data on the role of these differences in pattern as a function of ongoing thought. It may well be that we can begin to assign some relative quantitative weighting to certain strains of thought and that a method such as I have suggested may serve to establish hierarchies of difficulty or strain for individuals or for larger samples.

The Transition to Dreaming

In the course of examining the phenomenon of the stream of thought in myself, it became clear that my personal experience seemed to contradict reports emerging from the recent research on dreams. Accordingly, the following section is presented as an instance where research reports presented in objective fashion may benefit from evaluation in the light of phenomenal experience. To the extent that personal experience, not only evaluated as general impressions but examined more formally, offers data at variance with research reports, then a reinterpretation of general findings would appear desirable. Either the "objective" results are partly artifactual or a greater degree of individual difference in pattern exists than had been anticipated from the available data. Personal experience systematically examined or reported can scarcely provide a basis for decision in science, but it can raise serious questions about the generality of available group data and can suggest new hypotheses that can take into account such phenomena.

The exciting reports of the cyclical character of dreams by Dement and his collaborators (Dement and Kleitman, 1957; Oswald, 1962) seemed clearly to contradict the notion that there is an ongoing stream of activity even in early sleep since dreaming, as measured by electrophysiological criteria such as eye-movement measures and awakenings, was practically never found immediately after the subject fell asleep. More recent data by Foulkes (1962), however, have limited this generalization, suggesting that some qualitative differences in vividness and "dreaminess" of content are evident in awakenings at times when the established electrophysiological criteria of dreaming are not met. The data from the electrophysiological studies of sleep have found no evidence of rapid eye movements upon onset of sleep and no indications of dreaming until perhaps three quarters of an hour after onset of sleep.

As a moderately frequent dreamer (in the sense of frequency of recall), I had often noted that I dreamed immediately upon falling asleep. I knew this because of external evidence of the lapse of time. For example, my wife and I have observed that on occasions when one of us falls asleep before the other while conversing at bedtime and then is suddenly aroused, he or she will often make an incomprehensible retort to the other's remarks. What has happened is that the one who has fallen asleep has had a brief dream and upon being suddenly awakened by the annoyed partner has made a response not to the unheard conversation but to stimulus material in the dream. Mintz (1948), following a similar observation, had sought to link this response to a sleep stimulus to certain characteristics of schizophrenic behavior in the waking state.

Extending this observation to other situations, I realized that on occasions where I had fallen asleep during lectures or dull administrative meetings and had awakened abruptly, I almost invariably recalled a dream. The dream, although brief, generally seemed as remote in content and as odd as any dream I might recall upon awakening after a night's sleep. I had also noticed dreams occurring on a few occasions at large parties where I was drowsy. While actually talking to someone I might fall asleep in mid-sentence, awaken abruptly and make a bizarre comment, notice the puzzled looks on my friends' faces, and hastily seek to tie in the unrelated remark to the previous waking flow of conversation. What had obviously occurred again was a verbal response to the dream stimulus which was of course wholly out of context. Questioning my companions subsequently made it clear that only a few seconds had elapsed and that there had been no awareness on their part that I had fallen asleep.

The phenomena I have been describing seem to me indistinguishable from the usual night dream. It should be noted, however, that I am not referring to those strange experiences occasionally reported as occurring at the onset of sleep or upon awakening in the morning, the hypnagogic or hypnopompic phenomena. These phenomena seem more specifically sensory phenomena closely tied to the peripheral physiology of transitions to and from sleep and are phenomenally fairly readily distinguishable from the ongoing, visually oriented narrative of a dream to which I am referring (Oswald, 1962).

I began making inquiries of others. At the phenomenal level about fifty people to whom I have spoken all agreed that they observed dreams occurring under circumstances similar to those I have described, that is, during brief catnaps in public situations or during conversations while in bed.

Spurred by this seemingly widespread occurrence, I tried a more systematic self-observation. I had long been in the practice of taking late afternoon naps, particularly when I had a heavy and late-hour schedule of patients. I generally found that I could fall asleep quickly and would almost invariably awaken with the consciousness of a dream. I therefore began setting my alarm to awaken me at various predetermined, ran-

domized intervals to ascertain whether or not I would
recall a dream. I used five intervals—of three minutes,
five minutes, fifteen minutes, thirty minutes, and an
hour. Immediately upon being awakened I made a
note of whether or not I recalled a dream, and, if
possible, the actual content in sketchy form.

My findings were quite clear-cut. I recalled a dream
after all but one awakening, and that after a five-
minute interval. Clear recollection of the detailed content was less common, but I found no relationship
between clarity and interval of sleep. The contents of
the dreams I could record were typical of my usual
dream patterns. The material generally proved susceptible to analysis in terms of personal problems, unresolved issues, and the usual make-up of dreams. As
far as I could tell, there was rarely any continuity with
the events or thoughts immediately preceding sleep.
The major finding was that vivid dreaming did occur
within minutes or seconds of my falling asleep, since
in the three- and five-minute intervals some time must
have been consumed before I actually was asleep.

The content of the dreams after the briefer intervals
tended on the whole to be less detailed than the material recalled after a longer nap. Fairly extended dreams
did occur during five minutes, however, such as one in
which I found myself returning to work at a hospital I
had been employed at before but under different circumstances, conversing with a number of colleagues,
and meeting a series of somewhat bizarre crises. The
content bore no relation to any thought I could recall
from that day but was influenced by some snatches of
conversation from the previous day. Of course, upon
analysis, it brought out a number of significant con-

cerns in my life which were stated in metaphorical or symbolic fashion in the dream.

Since few or no rapid eye movements are reported at the onset of sleep, it can be argued that my dreams may not have involved active movement. I checked this point by examining content more carefully and while vigorous vertical or horizontal movements are not generally characteristic of my dreams, they did occur in some of my dreams in the experiment. For example, one dream involved my traveling on escalators and moving sidewalks (such as the ones at the New York World's Fair) and being unable to get on to the right one—for example, trying to get to the General Motors' stairway but finding that I was always going up or down on General Foods'! The reader may interpret as he wishes.

The occurrence of moderately extended dreams with rich symbolic personal content emphasizes my observation that the dreams I have noted immediately after falling asleep do not have the qualities ascribed to hypnagogic phenomena but represent genuine dreams. Except for being somewhat shorter, they seem quite representative of the general pattern of my own dreams and, for that matter, comparable in structural qualities to the dreams reported in psychoanalytic literature. In the instances where I have had an opportunity to be wired up for EEG study during afternoon naps, I have had dreams with no EEG evidence of rapid eye movements. It has, of course, been more difficult to fall asleep under those conditions and, unfortunately, I have not been able to carry this out sufficiently frequently to develop a habitual pattern which would permit a more natural sleep pattern. An example of one dream was the vivid appearance of a woman, an Igorot whom I had photographed in the Philippine Islands, who approached me menacingly in a crouching position with hands extended. Although I recalled the dream vividly and we could identify subsequently approximately the time it had occurred from motor restlessness, recorded on the EEG machine before and after, no REMs (rapid eye movements) were evident.

From these experiences I have found it hard to avoid the conclusion that there exists a certain amount of fairly continuous preconscious associative activity which comes "conscious" as soon as sleep begins. This interpretation has just been supported by a recently published study by David Foulkes and Gerald Vogel (1965), who also studied mental activity at sleep onset with electrophysiological methods. They too found ample evidence of dreaming in the absence of rapid eye movements and during sleep-onset EEG patterns. The activity in this transitional period seems to me to be closely related to daydreaming but differs in that a conscious active intention and control of direction are usually absent.

The extremely consistent finding in my own case and the anecdotal reports of others strongly suggest that the conception of periodic dreaming with the initial dream coming after the dreamer has been asleep for some time is inaccurate. Ullman (1958) has argued that the dream represents the ongoing reverberatory activity of the brain under conditions where external stimulation is reduced and the more abstract mode of dealing with reality has been eliminated. The brain has not stopped active efforts at interpretation of stimuli, however, and what occurs is a response that is highly concrete, a refraction of ordinary waking thoughts through the prism of the visual image and sensation-oriented prism analogous to Pavlov's primary signalling system.

My own experience suggests that in the waking state a much greater focusing of attention and volitional control of thought direction are possible. Furthermore, waking thought is socialized, that is, geared to some extent to accord with certain environmental social demands, and it is also influenced by one's capacity for abstraction. At the same time, however, the active brain is forming many additional associations which can be easily ignored under conditions of high intellectual efficiency or, in Head's phrase, "central vigilance." When there is a temporary relaxation of such control, one can be more aware of fantasies and daydreams, and as sleep takes over, the same brain activity is immediately evident in dreams. As sleep deepens it is possible that dreaming disappears, only to recur with cyclical variations in arousal. We shall return to a discussion of this issue subsequently, but it seems likely that dreams and daydreams represent different points along a common continuum of ongoing cerebral activity.

Suggestions for Further Research

The methods described in this chapter seem generally applicable to a wider range of problems dealing with transitional features of consciousness, marginal thoughts, and differences in structure between daydreams and sleeping dreams. One ought to begin with a frequently observed personal experience and move from that to a systematic study of the phenomenon in oneself before attempting a study with other subjects. By using techniques of factorial design with prerandomized instructions on cards, one can avoid problems of self-selection or mood interference with a specific feature since the overall randomization with sufficient repetition can provide satisfactory statistical means for evaluating error variance. It may be argued that one's conscious participation in the experiment automatically alters the psychological situation from its "naturalistic" meaning. This psychological rough analogy to Heisenberg's indeterminacy principle in physics cannot really be avoided in any formal psychological study for which a person is a conscious participant. Reminiscence about the occurrence of the phenomena before the formal experiment may be of some help in evaluating gross changes as a result of formalization. An important methodological feature of any formal experiment of this type requires some habituation, however, before formal trials begin, since restlessness and extreme self-consciousness are more in evidence in the first few sessions of a self-experiment.

By prerandomizing assignments along various categories or times for setting alarms, by using pretested systems of rating content, frequency, or other variables, and by using tape-recorded verbal ratings or verbal accounts, it is possible to obtain relatively immediate reports with a minimum of complex questioning. This type of self-experiment can thus be changed into a more generalizable group experiment without losing valuable personal consistency data. Further examples of this technique of rating will be presented in connection with experimental studies relating inner experience to external stimulus demands, to be discussed below.

Some kinds of questions that call for exploration by a technique of this type may be cited briefly. How widespread is the experience of dreaming during brief catnaps or afternoon naps? (South Americans have informed me that dreaming during short siestas is widespread but no formal data are available.) To what extent can one detect continuity in content between the presleep thoughts or external experience (for example, the words of a lecturer or on a radio at one's bedside) and the dream content? In my own case the continuity I have reported has been in the sheer persistence of some type of mental activity, but there is a striking break in *content* between the waking thoughts and daydreams or the sleeping dream. On an overall basis, there is a marked structural similarity in my waking and sleeping fantasy with regard to the storylike, quasi-logical sequence. The whole issue of cognitive style is obviously relevant here. One might well check a number of issues concerning whether fantasy, either in frequency or in pattern, shows a greater degree of development in certain individuals than in others, or whether it is in fact a pervasive phenomenon that has gone unnoticed in less articulate persons only because they have not been asked to study this phenomenon in themselves.

Chapter

3

NORMATIVE STUDIES OF DAYDREAMING: QUESTIONNAIRE AND INTERVIEW METHODS

Let us next turn to an examination of some approaches to studying the characteristics of daydreaming in the general population of normal adults. Surprisingly, despite numerous individual anecdotal accounts of daydreams elicited in clinical practice, we have very little formal evidence of the extent and pattern of daydreaming among presumably normal persons in our society. Indeed, until such time as we can establish a more extensive base of information on the range of daydreaming for the "man in the street," our clinical interpretations of the possible malignant implications of rather bizarre fantasies remain on shaky ground.

The general air of privacy and embarrassment often associated with daydreaming in our society may well be expected to limit the effectiveness of direct inquiry techniques. Nevertheless, the early work of Jersild,

Markey, and Jersild (1933) and Green (1923), who interviewed children about fantasy behavior, and of Shaffer (1936) and Seeman (1951), who used a generalized daydream questionnaire technique with well-educated adults, has indicated that direct methods are worth pursuing. Often enough psychologists may too easily assume defensiveness on the part of normal persons and resort to indirect or disguised techniques before fully evaluating the possibilities of a direct method of eliciting information.

The questions one might seek to answer about daydreaming by means of questionnaire or interview include:

1. What is the frequency of daydreaming in various samples of the normal population?

2. What types or contents of daydreaming manifest themselves among normals?

3. Are there differences in the frequency or content of daydreaming as a function of sex, age, cultural background, educational level, marital status, and various other environmental parameters?

4. Is frequency of daydreaming associated with a particular set of personality characteristics or with specific patterns of development or identification with parental figures?

Some General Characteristics of Adult Daydreaming

One of the first steps in the general program of research on daydreams called for the development of questionnaire and interview schedules for administration to normal adults as a means of obtaining some

basic information on daydream frequency. Technical
details of the construction of the measuring instru-
ments are available elsewhere (Singer and McCraven,
1961; Singer and McCraven, 1962; Singer and Antrobus, 1963). Essentially the findings to be discussed in
this chapter represent an attempted integration of
results from a number of separate investigations primarily with questionnaires. The General Daydream
Questionnaire called for persons to indicate the frequency (on a six-point scale) with which they had
experienced each of a series of approximately one
hundred daydreams assembled into a scale by prior
research. Examples of the specific daydreams employed included:

> "I plan how to increase my income in the next
> year."
> "I have my own yacht and plan a cruise of the
> Eastern Seaboard."
> "As a child I imagined myself a great detec-
> tive."
> "I see myself in heaven and see myself trans-
> formed."
> "I suddenly find I can fly—to the amazement of
> passersby."
> "I see myself eating and drinking unusual deli-
> cacies at a great banquet."
> "I see myself in the arms of a warm and loving
> person who satisfies all my needs."
> "I picture an atomic bombing of the town I live
> in."
> "I see myself participating with wild abandon
> in a Roman orgy."

CONDITIONS FAVORABLE
TO DAYDREAMING

Let us consider first some of the results obtained from a sample of 240 presumably normal adults between ages 19 and 50, of at least college education, who come from a fairly widespread area in the United States (Singer and McCraven, 1961). It is noteworthy that 96 per cent of the respondents reported that they engage in some form of daydreaming daily. Their daydreams take the form of fairly clear images of people, objects, or events. Visual imagery is the predominant modality for fantasy. Daydreaming is reported to occur chiefly when one is alone. Items dealing with daydream planning for future actions and particularly interpersonal contacts are high in frequency. Most daydreaming is reported to occur shortly before sleep when the respondent is in bed. Daydreaming is least frequent upon awakening in the morning, during meals, and during sexual activity. Most people reported that they enjoy daydreaming and denied that it embarrasses them. Analysis of the questionnaire yields the general conclusion that daydreaming is a remarkably widespread common occurrence when people are alone and in restful motor states. It is a human function that chiefly involves resort to visual imagery and is strongly oriented towards future interpersonal behavior.

The daydreams that were ranked high in frequency by the largest percentage of persons are those that involve fairly practical immediate concerns. At the same time, a very high proportion of respondents also indicated frequent daydreams dealing with sexual satisfaction, altruistic concern, and unusual good fortune.

Items with high probability of occurrence in the future (for example, "vacation plans") and items of a more speculative or wishful nature ("inherit a million dollars," or "I think of what heaven . . . might be like") occur together with high frequency.

Inspection of the range of items with high frequencies in the entire questionnaire suggests that daydreaming cannot be equated with specifically wish-fulfilling ideation. It would appear more appropriate to look upon the content of daydreaming for this sample as reflecting attempts at exploring the future, as Freud suggested, through "trial actions" or through positing a variety of alternatives not specifically involving satisfactory outcomes. The predominant content of daydreams seems to reflect fairly practical concern with life situations, yet it is apparent that more speculative contents emerge. And it is of interest, incidentally, that more than a few subjects reported daydreams of relatively unconventional concern —such as Messianic fantasies, homosexual satisfaction, and family murder—as having occurred with some frequency.

Do any particular patterns characterize persons who show either extremely high or extremely low frequencies of reported fantasy?

Evaluation of the daydream content of the extreme groups suggests that on the whole the high frequency group subscribes to statements that are more fantastic or unlikely of occurrence, with both more wishful and, to a lesser extent, more anxious content. Heroic achievement, Messianic identification, and sensual gratification are all included. It seems clear that the high frequency of daydreaming group has available a dimension of experience along which any number of possible human behaviors can be played out with relative impunity.

SOME BACKGROUND CHARACTERISTICS ASSOCIATED WITH DAYDREAM FREQUENCY AND CONTENT

In the questionnaire studies that have been carried out with well over five hundred persons, no evidence has yet emerged to show that sex differences play a significant role in daydream frequency or in content— except for obvious items such as women's greater interest in fashion and men's in athletics or physical feats and heroics. Nor has marital status proved to be a factor in fantasy patterns.

Other background factors, however, do seem to have relationship to daydream frequency and content, and these will now be presented.

Age. A significant decline in reported daydreaming frequency emerges with age for this sample. The maximum daydreaming reported is between ages eighteen and twenty-nine, with decreasing frequency in the thirty to thirty-nine group, and with lowest reported frequency in persons aged forty to forty-nine. No really elderly individuals were included, however, and it remains a possibility that were items geared more toward the *past* and reminiscence, daydreaming would then show a higher reported frequency among the very old.

As for the decline in daydreaming frequency with age, there are several possible explanations. It seems likely that the increased responsibilities and family involvements of the older respondents leave little time

for solitude and the conditions necessary for daydreaming. A second possibility is that daydreaming is a
function that involves, even in its fantastic aspects,
some attitude towards the *probable*. Thus, as the persons in this group have moved from the late teens and
twenties, when they were full of plans and possibilities
and probably were receiving training towards long-
range goals, into the settled roles and more limited
range of career and family choices of middle age, then
the distant future beckons less and concerns are narrowed to current and near-future situations.

Speculating further, Lewin's analysis of the development of the personality and the increasing differentiation and crystallization of inner personal regions
and of reality levels (Lewin, 1946) suggests itself at
once. For the adolescent his limited experience has led
to a relatively minimal awareness of what he cannot
do or of what "the world" or his social environment
will prevent him from doing. While he may have
many activities in which he participates and is as
"busy" as the older person, he is less likely to be as
regulated by a narrow series of *obligated* behavior
within the scope of family situations or job responsibility. And he has less reason to be disillusioned about
the variety of aspirations. Thus the adolescent has
both more time and "imaginative life space" than the
adult for engaging in extensive fantasy behavior. We
shall discuss this at greater length in a subsequent
chapter.

Education and Socioeconomic Status. While one
might anticipate that education and one's degree of
exposure to the greatly diversified stimulus complex of
education would influence fantasy tendencies, we have
as yet no evidence on this point. We have not in this

general project had an opportunity to study persons from lower educational levels or persons of semi-skilled or unskilled labor backgrounds. Within our relatively homogeneous sample, however, no difference in daydreaming patterns emerged as a function of education differences. Because of the relatively restricted range in socioeconomic status, no findings emerged for that dimension, either. One might speculate that persons of limited education or lower socioeconomic status may be stimulated by television or movies to envision romantic fulfillments without, however, any awareness of the intermediate steps necessary for such goal attainments. In contrast, the middle-class youth, whose life is often structured from an early age in terms of a series of linked subgoals, may demonstrate a more realistic type of fantasy content. A personal communication by Dr. Kenneth Clark, based on his experience with Harlem adolescents in the Haryou Project, does indeed support the above assertion. These lower socioeconomic, poorly educated Negro youths showed initially very high fantasy goals which then seemed to prove frustrating and form the basis for a bitterness and despair.

Rural-Urban Background. The highest daydream frequency is reported by those persons raised in large cities, while respondents raised in suburbs report lowest daydream tendencies. Actually, our subjects from either large cities or rural areas contrast sharply with those from small towns or suburbs. While sociocultural groups may play some part here, no clear indication is available to explain this finding. One wonders, however, if city life and rural life do not in their own ways provide greater loneliness or periods of solitariness, whether wandering through the fields or sitting in the subway, than does suburban life, with its more organized activities and its emphasis on "together-ness."

Family Constellation. While the questionnaire and interview studies in the research program have not as yet sought extensive information about familial patterns, it has been possible to test one type of hypothesis that bears on the role of the family constellation or the pattern of relative maternal-paternal identification on the development of an extensive fantasy life. The data relevant to this hypothesis are drawn from two studies, both of which use the Daydream Questionnaire and a measure of parental identification, Oliner's Scale of Assumed Similarity to Parents (Singer and McCraven, 1961; Singer and Schonbar, 1961).

The disposition to engage in or fully report daydreaming may be viewed to some extent as a learned response which develops differentially as a function of certain patterns of early experience and of parent-child relationships. Of particular significance in its development appears to be the opportunity for identification with a benign parental figure under circumstances in which the parent frequently rewards the child for controlling its movements and emotions when there is a delay in satisfying some urgent desires or impulses (Singer, 1960). To some extent, mothers in our society tend to represent inhibition of impulses and also to foster aesthetic interest, while fathers represent action tendencies and the external environment. Closer identification with a mother figure would therefore appear particularly to be related to introspective tendencies.

In general, the data from the two studies cited above support this hypothesis. In the Singer-Schonbar

(1961) investigation in which only female subjects were involved, greater daydream frequency proved to be significantly associated with greater apparent similarity (based on self-ratings) to mother than to father. The women who reported more extensive daydreaming (and incidentally also recalled more night dreams) appeared to be more closely identified with their mothers. Women with infrequent daydreaming not only seemed closer to their fathers but also listed significantly more male figures or women associated with masculine activities as the historical or fictional persons they most emulated or admired. In general, similar evidence of greater maternal identification for high frequency daydreamers emerged for both male and female respondents on the Singer-McCraven (1961) study as well. These results are indeed intriguing and will be discussed more extensively in Chapter 4.

Sociocultural Background. Perhaps the most striking result obtained in the analysis of questionnaire responses was the finding of large differences between persons from differing subcultural groups in daydreaming frequency and content. In one study (Singer and McCraven, 1961), respondents were categorized according to the following subcultural backgrounds (both parents): Negro, Jewish, Anglo-Saxon, mixed parentage, and other (small samples of German, Polish, and so on). The Negro and Jewish groups showed the highest daydream frequencies, and the Anglo-Saxons the lowest.

These intriguing findings on sociocultural group differences in reported frequency of daydreaming prompted a more extensive examination of this issue with another sample. Formal experimental hypotheses derived from an examination of the interaction between the sociocultural impact on development and its relationship to daydreaming (Singer and McCraven, 1962) were erected for testing. Following an analysis of possible parental influence on the development of daydreaming, it was felt that on the cultural level one might expect that in families where the modal constellation emphasizes a patriarchal or matriarchal pole or where for some reason one of the parents is more available for identification purposes, the relative development of fantasy versus action tendencies might be crudely predictable. Some support for this point has come from studies with schizophrenic males (Opler and Singer, 1956; Singer and Opler, 1956).

A further factor to be considered along a widening sphere of cultural impact on daydream development was the relative acceptance or emphasis on such fantasy play activity on the part of the subculture in which the child develops. In a culture where such types of parent-child contact are fostered, one might expect greater enrichment of the daydream life of the child. These patterns go beyond the immediate family, however, and to some extent characterize the reactions of peer groups and non-familial cultural authorities as well, thus reinforcing the social role of the child in relation to imaginative tendencies.

There remains still another level of influence which may foster daydreaming, the sociological. To some extent daydreaming represents one medium by which a person may explore his environment or "life-space" without committing himself to action. It is possible that membership in an upwardly mobile social group might produce a greater tendency to daydreaming. Just as a football player looks for an opening between the shifting mass of men, the person seeking advancement in social status seeks out avenues of fulfillment. Often, too, he is doing more than that, for, by exploring a variety of possible outcomes, he may arrive at new combinations of means-end awareness or possibly generate new needs. For a social group that has attained a relatively stable or secure status, the future may be less intriguing or demanding of imaginary exploration. Value differences in past versus future orientation for upper- and middle-class American college students in stories told to Thematic Apperception Test pictures were indeed found by McArthur (1955).

Of the various subcultural groups that reflect some reasonably definable modal patterns, six were available for study on the basis of data obtained in the course of the daydream project. The hypotheses called for differences in daydreaming frequency and content between samples of Anglo-Saxons (Old Americans), Germans, Irish, Italians, Jews, and Negroes. In terms of immigration waves and relatively assimilated or socially stable positions in the United States, the order of these groups from most to least secure should be reflected in a parallel increase in frequency of reported daydreaming. Thus daydreaming frequency was predicted from most to least frequent for Negro, Italian, Jewish, Irish, German, and Anglo-Saxon, in approximately that order.

In order to test these hypotheses, the Daydream Questionnaire was administered to approximately four hundred college and graduate students in the New York City area. From this group it was possible to select representatives of the six subcultural groups who fell within a common age category (twenty to thirty) and who could also be equated for socioeconomic status and educational level. A measure of As-

sumed Similarity to Parental Figures was also administered and suitable technical controls for cultural
background, educational level, and other factors were
employed (Singer and McCraven, 1962).

The results of this study strongly confirmed the experimental hypotheses. The various groups differed
among themselves in both frequency and content pattern of their reported daydreaming on the questionnaire. The groups arranged in order of daydreaming
frequency from highest to lowest score were Italian,
Negro, Jewish, Irish, Anglo-Saxon, and German.
These six groups formed an obvious clustering into
two groups of three: the Italian, Negro, and Jewish,
representing groups still relatively recently immigrant
and upwardly mobile, showed very similar scores,
while the other three groups, which have a more secure status in the United States, all scored much lower
on the daydream frequency scale. Comparing the daydream frequency scores for each group of three yields
a significant difference that clearly supports the sociological hypothesis. The Italian, Jewish, and Negro subjects thus report significantly more frequent daydreaming than do those subjects of Irish, German, and
Anglo-Saxon background.

On the Parental Identification Questionnaire, the
Italian, Jewish, and Negro respondents also reveal
themselves to be least like their fathers in their behavioral preferences. They also perceive their fathers
as being quite different from what they feel would be
their own ideal self-images. These results generally
confirm the hypothesis that persons who show less
identification with their fathers or who perceive their
fathers as far removed from the standards they have

set for themselves, also report greater daydream activity.

Turning next to the specific content categories in which the subcultural groups differ in their daydreaming, a number of interesting findings emerge. The Negro respondents show a high degree of relatively concrete, realistic daydreams, while the Jewish and Anglo-Saxon groups score at the opposite extreme, minimizing reliance on highly materialistic fantasies. Significant group differences fail to emerge for highly improbable daydreams, although the Irish subjects showed by far the greatest resort to these mystical, other-worldly, or otherwise fantastical fantasies—a carry-over of leprechaun influences, no doubt. No significant group differences emerged on daydreams classified as involving direct or overt aggressive or destructive drives, but when modified, partially controlled aggression is considered, significant group differences do occur, with the Irish showing by far the highest and the Anglo-Saxon the lowest scores in these categories. Most curious is the fact that the Negro, Jewish, and Italian groups are particularly high on total erotic drive fantasies.

Some interesting results within each subcultural group also emerged. The Negroes' general daydream pattern indicated considerable preoccupation with fairly concrete sensual gratifications and material security. Their pattern seemed grossly to reflect the middle-class Negro concern with achievement of material satisfaction that has been described by Frazier (1957). Of course these data were gathered before the sixties, when the Civil Rights movement became so central a concern of educated Negroes.

No striking trends emerged for the Jewish group, but the Italians, with their concern about death and afterlife, showed some of the fatalistic cultural value reported by Strodtbeck (1958). The Irish in their daydreams alternated passionate or dramatic-heroic fantasies with religious preoccupations. This seems somewhat in keeping with previous reports of the ambivalence in the Irish between a rich fantasy and their greater religious orientation (Opler and Singer, 1956; Woods, 1956). The Germans showed no special content pattern except for a low general frequency of reported daydreaming. The respondents of Anglo-Saxon background tended to be least willing to speculate imaginally or to give free play to sensual interests or strong affects; at the same time, they showed a greater apparent self-satisfaction than the other groups.

It is worth noting that while daydream frequency seems related to upward mobility, the content of the daydreams is not limited to achievement or material acquisition. In general, one may say that upward mobility invites a wide variety of fantasies rather than simply those specific to the change in social status. For the Negro subjects, the particular fantasies seem to mirror the pattern of concern with security and possession or need gratification rather than achievement, which Frazier (1957) has described. For other groups the pattern is less clear. This result may reflect the special problems of the Negroes as members of a particularly visible minority with so recent a history of slavery.

The assimilation process of subcultural groups into the dominant white Anglo-Saxon Protestant American culture (Woods, 1956) seems to involve a gradual decrease and blurring of the variety and richness of imagination. The data so far available cannot conclusively document this, but the relative infrequency and lack of uniqueness in daydreaming patterns for the German and Anglo-Saxon groups raises some intriguing questions. Does the lower frequency and variety of fantasy in the assimilated groups represent a movement towards health and effective action, rather than indecision and anxious speculation? Or, does it, perhaps, represent a denial of inner richness and introspection and a movement in the direction of conformity and a limitation of individuality? Whatever the answer, it seems clear that research on the daydream patterns of various subcultural or social-class groups affords many interesting possibilities on the border areas of psychology, anthropology, and sociology.

Cognitive and Personality Correlates of Daydreaming Frequency and Content

So far we have focused attention on background factors associated with frequency of reported daydreaming. What of the factors *within* the person, so to speak, which seem to occur concurrently with a disposition to frequent fantasy behavior? The data to be presented in this section are drawn chiefly from two published investigations (Singer and Antrobus, 1963; Singer and Schonbar, 1961) and some hitherto unreported work carried out as part of the daydream project. In this presentation the emphasis will be not so much on research methodology but upon some of the major findings and indications for further effort.

One question which seems fairly obvious involves the relationship of daydream predisposition and the general cognitive approach of the individual. To what extent does the tendency towards fantasy behavior reflect intelligence or specialized perceptual or thinking abilities? The data to be presented represent only a beginning of a much-needed systematic exploration of these questions.

INTELLIGENCE AND
DAYDREAM FREQUENCY

It seems obvious that if elements of enriched vocabulary, reading experience, and combinatory skills are involved in fantasy, then there ought to be some relationship between daydreaming and general intelligence. Yet what data we do have suggest that the association between intelligence and daydreaming frequency is a subtle one. There is, for example, ample evidence (Sarason, 1944) that even moderately mentally retarded children and adults manifest fantasy activities at least in response to picture stimuli. Within the samples hitherto studied by questionnaire techniques, the relatively limited range of subjects (most being college-educated or better) has also restricted the range of possible intelligence test scores. For the well-educated women in the study by Singer and Schonbar, no significant relationship was found between intelligence (measured by the Lorge-Thorndike scale) and daydream frequency. In the Singer-Antrobus study of one hundred college freshmen, there was again only the very slightest relationship between daydream frequency or any particular pattern of daydreaming and the intelligence measures. It would appear, then, that for a well-educated, above average intelligence group, the *degree* of intelligence does not especially influence frequency of daydreaming or any special pattern of fantasy. What we do not know is whether this lack of relationship would still obtain if we were able to study a full range of intellectually diversified adults.

DIVERGENT PRODUCTIVITY AND DAYDREAM FREQUENCY

Even if intelligence in its more general form is unrelated to fantasy, one might well anticipate that particular tendencies toward varied kinds of thought would be associated with a disposition towards daydreaming. It would appear likely that a person who shows a great deal of what might be called ideational or verbal fluency would be likely to daydream more often since, after all, the frequent daydreamer, according to the questionnaire studies in the project, shows a willingness to entertain a greatly varied range of fantasies. In the Singer-Antrobus investigation with college freshmen, a large number of measures of what Guilford (1959) has called "Divergent Productivity" were administered, along with various daydream frequency, content, and structure scales. In general, the results did not show any consistent evidence that daydream frequency was accompanied by abilities to produce with rapidity great varieties of material—such as plot titles, various uses of brick, and word fluency. Intuitively, despite the lack of evidence from this study, one cannot avoid the impression that persons who daydream frequently should be likely to produce a greater variety of cognitive or original material. It may be that the persons with considerable ideational tendency are *slower* to respond and do less well on timed tests because there is more of a response to internally produced stimuli, which slows down reaction. If that is the case, and the work on Rorschach measures of fantasy (Singer, 1960) suggests it may be, further study with untimed tests might be a necessary step to clarify this issue.

CURIOSITY, CREATIVITY, AND DAYDREAMING

One might also anticipate that persons engaging in frequent daydreaming would be characterized by a considerable exploratory tendency, at least at the ideational level, and perhaps by creativity in their storytelling abilities. Measures of curiosity about personal and interpersonal events were included in the Singer-Antrobus investigation. The general daydreaming frequency pattern which emerged in that study did relate to curiosity about interpersonal events. The Singer-Schonbar, Singer-McCraven (1961), and Singer (1961) studies with adults and children found evidence of frequent general daydreaming by those persons whose written or dictated stories were rated by judges as most original or creative. While none of these relationships are very high, they appear consistently in various studies with differing samples, e.g., Helson (1965). Frequent daydreaming may well involve a combination of curiosity about people and willingness to try out original combinations of story material. It remains an open question, however, whether similar results could be obtained if measures of creativity in nonliterary activities—for example, music or science, were available. In the Singer-Antrobus study, a pattern of daydreaming characterized by objective, controlled content did prove to be linked with curiosity about events and nature rather than about people.

THE RELATIONSHIP OF REPORTED DAYDREAM FREQUENCY TO ANXIETY AND EMOTIONAL STABILITY

Moving from more cognitively oriented variables to those more related to personality tendencies, we are confronted with the widespread American stereotype that frequent daydreaming is a symptom of neurotic tendencies. The first inventories designed to screen out the emotionally disturbed generally included an item such as "I daydream frequently." Even quite recently in interpreting a set of items which clustered on the Minnesota Multiphasic Personality Inventory, Welsh (1956) indicated that the occurrence of a "daydream" item in the group was evidence to support describing the cluster as representing *neuroticism*.

One step in evaluating the possible emotional correlates of daydreaming has been to compare scores for normal respondents on the Daydream Questionnaire with their scores on measures of anxiety or emotional instability. The evidence from a number of studies in the general research program indicates that daydreaming frequency does correlate positively at moderately high levels with questionnaire measures of anxiety, including Welsh's A scale (Singer and Schonbar, 1961) and Cattell's Anxiety scale (Singer and Rowe, 1962; Rowe, 1963). This would suggest that persons reporting more frequent daydreams also describe themselves as more anxious, sensitive, and fearful. Yet is this the same as being seriously disturbed emotionally? According to Cattell (1957), conscious anxiety as measured by his scale is a normal phenomenon. Persons who are not clinically neurotic may score high on it—reflecting their willingness to tolerate consciously the fears that others experience only through psychosomatic symptoms, phobic avoidance, or drinking and addictive patterns.

More subtle evidence on this point came in the Antrobus and Singer (1963) investigation in which a number of daydream scales were studied by the factor analytic method. Here it was found that the more general pattern of daydreaming could be analyzed into several patterns, one generally reflecting broad and wishful fantasy activity, another predominantly associated with fearful daydreams or fantasies preoccupied with the body. The latter daydream pattern was indeed associated with measures of emotional instability (the Maudsley scale and the Guilford-Zimmerman scale) which had been standardized comparing known patients with normals. Moreover, Rowe (1963) when applying the scales to normals undergoing stress found that the general daydream frequency scale was associated with lower heart rate and relatively little autonomic arousal. It seems likely that only one pattern of fantasy is associated with serious disturbance, while the more general daydreaming scale reflects anxiety only insofar as the daydream and anxiety scales may both be reflecting the daydreamers' greater self-sensitivity, willingness to experience ideation consciously, and a general self-awareness. Indeed, in the Singer-Schonbar study, the high frequency daydreamers (on the general scale) showed such a "self-awareness" pattern; they recalled more of their night dreams, revealed less tendency to lie or repress thoughts (Minnesota Multiphasic Lie and R scales), as well as more anxiety on the Welsh A scale. The impression gained is less one of neurotic, disturbed persons than one of persons willing to see themselves in temporal or spatial perspective and to engage in some form of imaginative living. In contrast, persons who limit their fantasy activity more specifically to fearful thoughts and somatic preoccupations seem more likely to be the ones who show evidence of clinical manifestations of neuroticism.

PATTERNS OF DAYDREAMING

As one examines the nature of daydreaming more carefully through questionnaire and interview techniques, a variety of patterns of fantasy become discernible. The Singer-Antrobus (1963) study sought to explore some of these patterns by developing a variety of scales of daydreaming and an interview technique which could then be administered along with personality measures and other scales to ascertain specific styles of daydreaming. Seven fairly clear patterns emerged from this analysis, which is described in technical detail in the Singer-Antrobus (1963) monograph, and they are briefly presented below.

General Daydreaming. This pattern (technically speaking, a factor) suggests a tendency to have many diverse types of daydreams of high frequency and is associated also with curiosity about others. It resembles the general scale used in the earlier studies described in this chapter.

Self- Recriminating Daydreaming. Here the pattern

of daydreams reflects a somewhat obsessional, verbally expressive pattern associated with negative emotional reactions such as guilt, depression, and repetitive themes. It seems to be a type of imaginative reaction characteristic of obsessional personalities in which conscience and self-recrimination play an important role. Certainly the indications are that daydreams need not be only wishful or "drive-reducing" but may increase emotional reactions.

Objective, Controlled Thoughtfulness. This pattern is characterized by a controlled, objective approach to inner experience, reflective but not fantastical. The person who would score high on the scales making up this cluster might be a "thinking man" who wastes little time in idle fancy but who is far from an extrovert; indeed, he relies heavily on thought for problem solution and somewhat more scientific or abstract speculation. This pattern is linked to masculinity, emotional stability, and curiosity about nonhuman features of the world.

Poorly Controlled Kaleidoscopic Daydreams. The person scoring high on this pattern characterizes himself as showing marked distractibility, depression, self-debasement, easy boredom, and fleeting, vague thoughts. One feels that for such persons memories, perceptions, imaginal representations of emotion, and fragmentary associations flit more or less uncontrollably across their consciousness, producing a somewhat chaotic and distracting effect.

Neurotic, Self-conscious Daydreaming. This pattern has already been mentioned. It involves egocentric preoccupations and obsessive rumination over bodily reactions, with a lack of scope or richness of daydreaming content despite a great deal of responsiveness to inner processes. The general pattern most resembles the body-centered rumination that characterizes anxiety neuroses.

Autistic Daydreaming. This cluster most strongly suggests a more bizarre, "primary process" type of daydreaming, a breakthrough into consciousness of normally dissociated material. It reflects the kind of "dreamy," poorly controlled quality of inner experience often reported by schizoid individuals. It may be an early indication of a potential psychotic breakdown, but no evidence to support this belief is yet available.

Enjoyment of Daydreaming. Persons who score high on the scales comprising this factor would be characterized by their generally positive attitude toward daydreams. They show a healthful acceptance and enjoyment of daydreams and make use of inner experience for both pleasure and problem solution.

In general, even with the somewhat diverse factors described above, the analysis of the scales suggests the existence of a deeper, more general pattern of self-awareness or introspective behavior. At one end of this dimension of inner experience one finds the person given to extremely fantastic, fanciful daydreams, while at the other end the pattern suggests a considerably controlled, orderly, and objective type of daydreaming. The analogy to C. P. Snow's contrast (1959) of the "literary-humanist'" scholar and the physical scientist–engineer thinker comes to mind. Both extremes represent responsiveness to internally produced cognitive experiences quite different from the extrovert's push for direct perceptual and physical contact with the environment. It is of particular interest that both poles of this dimension of daydreaming are also associated with a measure of curiosity differing chiefly in the relative interpersonal-impersonality of reported interests. Persons emphasizing control of their thought processes tend also to be curious about natural events or the physical world; by contrast, the more fanciful daydreamers appear more curious about people and their motives or characteristics.

Suggestions for Further Research

Results with the use of questionnaires have been encouraging, considering the pitfalls of conscious deception, response set, and unreliability. Yet the rather considerable material summarized above from the questionnaire studies only points the way to much more that needs to be done in understanding the nature of individual differences in daydreaming patterns or the various dimensions of fantasy thought and their relation to cognitive skills or personality characteristics. We have so far almost no information on the daydreaming frequency or pattern of working-class adults or adolescents or of the fantasy patterns of the aged (although a study of this group is in preparation as part of the author's research program at this writing). The sociocultural group differences reported represent small samples and, again, are drawn from middle-class respondents. Technical problems such as the comparability of questionnaires for younger adolescents or children or persons of lower intelligence or education have not yet been dealt with.

The choice of other pertinent variables for inclusion in any correlational study is an intriguing one. One might well repeat this type of investigation using projective methods, as well as daydream question-naires and interviews, to ascertain fantasy. Other types of variables might be considered. Measures of cognitive style, such as the leveler-sharpener, field-dependent or independent, sensitizer-represser, or cognitive-complexity variables might yield interesting results.

Finally, the work on individual differences and personality dimensions has not dealt with the issue of pathological patterns of daydreaming. There are as yet no formal studies using the questionnaire or related techniques with markedly deviant adults or adolescents. One might predict a somewhat different patterning of the obtained dimensions with schizophrenics, for example. It may be that, despite common reference to the "private world" of the psychotic, the hospitalized schizophrenic may show less frequent and more impoverished daydreaming than the "normal." This issue will be dealt with at a more speculative level later; the fact remains that despite many theoretical articles or case-history investigations that touch on the issue, systematic study of the frequency and structure of daydreaming in the mentally ill remains to be done.

Chapter

4

EXPERIMENTAL STUDIES OF THE ADAPTIVE ROLE OF DAYDREAMING AND FANTASY

The work described in previous chapters has sought to establish some of the broader bases in factual information from which a more precise theory of daydreaming can be constructed. Turning now to the functional role of daydreaming in the economy of the personality, we shall touch more directly on important theoretical issues in psychology. Indeed, almost the only theorizing about the phenomena of daydreaming stems from the attempt of Freud to come to grips with the motivational properties of fantasy. Following a brief presentation of Freud's notions, as modified by some of his followers, we shall examine some of the evidence from research that bears on the issue of the relation of drives to daydreams and fantasy.

The Psychoanalytic Theory of Thought and Delayed Gratification

Among Sigmund Freud's greatest contributions to psychology were his efforts to formulate a conception of the relation of thought to instinct and adaptation. Freud sought to explain how the human being, dominated initially by pleasure-strivings (hunger, thirst, or sexual contact), can learn to defer the direct expressions of these drives in the interest of a more adaptive response pattern, since, except for the very young infant, gratification is rarely immediately available. How does the child's perceptual and motor apparatus learn to account for the realities of an external world where all needs cannot at once be fulfilled?

In effect, the early psychoanalytic position on fantasy proposed that all thought or imagination grew out of suppressed desires. Indeed, Freud went so far as to state in his paper on the poet and daydreaming that, "Happy people never make fantasies, only unsatisfied ones do" (Freud, 1962a). As elaborated by Rapaport (1951), Freud hypothesized that the transition from primary (associative, prelogical) to secondary process (organized, abstract) thought, or, in effect, from an *id*-dominated psychic topography to one in which the ego could be differentiated, came through the medium of the hallucinatory imagery of the child. A hungry child, in the absence of immediate gratification or the presence of Mama, automatically hallucinates the image of breast or bottle, since what is wished for occurs at once in primary process thought. The occurrence of the image has a temporarily satisfying value, however, and gradually the child learns that he

need not thrash around or spill over into violent cry-
ing or fruitless motor activity but that thinking about
the gratification is at least releasing enough so that he
can stall until mother's appearance.

In terms of energy concepts, then, Freud postulated
that thought and fantasy discharge small quantities of
energy and in this fashion permit delay and experimental action. This partially drive-reducing character
of thought decreases the pressure on the child and
opens the way for planning, organization of behavior,
and the synthetic and defensive capacities which are
conceptualized as the ego.

Neither Freud nor Rapaport, however, has dealt in
detail with the manner by which the hallucinated
image occurs in the first place nor with the way in
which the "hallucination" is internalized as daydreaming or fantasy thought. One might speculate that
Werner's sensory-tonic theory (see p. 84) might serve
as a link here, the checked motor impulses of the child
making him more susceptible to motion in the environment, and lacking that, to the re-creation of
movement through recall of the previously satisfying
acts associated with gratification.

More recent developments in psychoanalytic ego
psychology have emphasized the fact that ego functions such as thought, language, and motor skills may
derive energy from sources not specifically related to
libidinal conflicts. Indeed, Hartmann (1958) has suggested that fantasy itself need not arise only out of
frustration or deferred gratification, but may serve
adaptive functions for the organism from the start,
powered by an autonomous energy source. Nevertheless, the earlier conception of fantasy as involving a
partial drive-discharge, growing out of frustrated

impulse, and serving as a defense mechanism (Anna Freud, 1937) or catharsis, remains the most widespread view and has influenced some interesting research explorations.

Let us now examine some patterns of research on fantasy that exemplify this conception of the defensive or cathartic function of imaginative phenomena. We shall begin with some relevant research based not specifically on daydreaming but on fantasy responses made to the ambiguous stimuli of the projective techniques in psychological testing.

Rorschach's Human Movement Response: The Inverse Relation of Imagination and Motility

In their approach to the study of imagination and daydreaming, an initial area explored by workers in this field was the relationship between certain variables in the Rorschach Psychodiagnostic Method and imagination and motor activity. About fifty years ago, in experimenting with individual patterns of reaction to various inkblots, Herman Rorschach (1942) made an interesting observation. Persons who responded frequently to inkblots by saying they might represent human beings in action ("Two men bowing, a woman with arms upraised doing a Spanish dance," and so on) presented a contradictory pattern of behavior. They were less overtly active, more controlled in their movements, or perhaps awkward physically. On the other hand, they were likely to be persons with considerable imagination, much given to inner living or attention to their own thoughts or daydreams. Although he was much struck by this observation and felt it a most important outcome of his inkblot studies, Rorschach did not attempt to develop a theoretical formulation about this triadic relationship of human-movement perception in inkblots, inhibited overt motility, and imaginative tendencies.

Despite general clinical agreement concerning the inverse relation of the human movement response (M) to overt motility and its direct relation to imagination, no formal experimental work attempted to test this observation until well into the 1940's. At that time the late Heinz Werner, a distinguished investigator in developmental psychology, observed that Rorschach's findings exemplified a perceptual theory which Werner himself had proposed. Werner's (1945) sensory-tonic theory of motion perception emphasized the body's tonicity as the dynamic link between muscular activity and perception. He showed in various experiments that alteration of body position affected perceptual response. He also demonstrated that retarded children who differed characteristically in their type of overt movement also differed in perception of motion or in movement responses to Rorschach inkblots. The endogenous mentally retarded, who were generally more controlled or phlegmatic in motility, showed significantly more Rorschach movement responses and lower thresholds for stroboscopically or tachistoscopically presented motion than did the hyperactive, exogenous mentally retarded.

Meltzoff, Singer, and Korchin (1953) carried this experimental approach further with a study which demonstrated that persons experimentally required to inhibit natural movement subsequently increased their human movement responses to the inkblots. Persons who showed numerous M responses also were better able to inhibit writing speed. Singer, Meltzoff, and Goldman (1952) found that Rorschach M responses increased after subjects were required to "freeze in place" for a period of time. Subsequently, a series of studies summarized in Singer (1960) demonstrated that persons who showed more M responses were likely to be able to inhibit motility; showed more deliberation in problem-solving, Porteus Maze performance, and more ability to delay in time estimation; were less active during solitary enforced waiting periods; were less likely to use gestures in defining verbs; or, in the case of mental patients, were less likely to be described by nurses or attendants as overactive on the wards.

These findings thus afford considerable support to Rorschach's original observation of the inverse relationship of overt motility and perception of movement on the inkblots. Somewhat less directly they support Werner's sensory-tonic theory, although Werner's formulations apply chiefly to perception and have not been extended to the study of imagination (Werner and Wapner, 1952). The relationship of the M response to imaginative behavior, daydreaming, or "creative intelligence" (as Rorschach also put it) remains to be explored.

One approach to measuring imaginative tendencies has been to score stories told to Thematic Apperception Test pictures for degree of creativity or for what Weisskopf (1950) termed "transcendence," the ability to include elements in a story that go beyond mere description of the immediate content of the picture. Thus, a story told to Card I of the TAT (a boy gazing at a violin) which merely described in detail the boy's appearance and the shading of the card would receive a minimal score for transcendence. A story which obviously introduced characters, time dimensions, and locations not actually represented on the card, seems clearly a more imaginative one, with a higher transcendence score.

Employing such criteria of imagination, investigators have indeed found support for some degree of relationship between Rorschach's M response and TAT measures of imagination, summarized in Singer (1960). Persons rated by observers as imaginative or having considerable inner life also show tendencies to produce more M responses (Barron, 1955). King (1960) found that persons with more frequent M responses showed greater interpersonal awareness and sensitivity. Brenner, in an unpublished study, found that persons instructed to adopt a creative attitude were more likely to give Rorschach M responses, and Bruel, in another unpublished experiment, found a greater number of M responses in the Rorschach records of literature students than in those of ballet students. Goldberger and Holt (1961) reported that persons in a sensory-deprivation experiment who showed capacity for extended thought devoted to topics other than the immediate experimental situation also gave considerably more Rorschach movement responses.

A crucial link in the chain of relating M to fantasy processes and daydreaming came in a study by Page (1957). Employing a questionnaire listing of daydreams quite similar to the type of questionnaire developed later by Singer and McCraven (1961), Page compared frequency of reported daydreaming to a number of Rorschach variables. Only the number of M responses proved to be significantly associated with daydream frequency. A really critical study linking Rorschach M to perceptual responses, daydreaming,

TAT measures of imagination, and measures of delay and inhibition remains to be done, although Singer, Wilensky, and McCraven (1956) found some evidence of such a patterning in an investigation with schizophrenic patients.

Pending such a comprehensive study, the evidence linking Rorschach M responses to motor inhibition or delaying capacity and to measures of imaginativeness seems moderately convincing. There does seem to have existed at the turn of the century a kind of *Zeitgeist* which pervaded the thought of persons otherwise as different as Dewey, Freud, Washburn, and E. B. Holt, concerning the inverse relationship between thought and action (Singer, 1955). The most specific statement that related the inhibition of motility to the development of a sustained tendency toward imagination seemed to be Freud's conception, outlined above, concerning the role of thought in partial drive discharge or catharsis. Thus Rorschach's observation and the experimental data which generally support it would seem to be consistent with psychoanalytic theory (Singer, 1955).

If we examine the relationship of the Rorschach M response to the psychoanalytic theory more closely, however, the connection of theory and empirical results is less certain. What the Rorschach results best suggest is that some well-developed cognitive style linking controlled motility and imagination does appear to exist. It is less certain that the drive-reducing characteristics of thought or fantasy can be a sufficient explanation for such a crystallized personality pattern. The increase in M after inhibition of motion, while supportive of Werner's theory, cannot be used to support Freud's concept unless it were shown that after producing the M responses the subjects were now less inclined

towards motility than they were before inhibition.
Such data have not been reported with the Rorschach.

In view of the relatively large number of studies
supporting the tie between inhibition or delaying
capacity, motion perception, and imagination, and the
findings of Page (1957) that M and reported daydream
frequency are positively associated, an intriguing avenue for further study is opened. We need more evidence of how M and daydream characteristics are
linked, and we need to be able to specify whether it is
human movement alone or all types of movement responses to the blots that are associated with fantasy;
the data are not clear on this point. Recall that the
Singer and Antrobus (1963) study (cited in the previous chapter) found two poles of a general daydreaming factor, one personally oriented, one impersonal.
Roe (1952) in her studies of the Rorschach responses
of scientists found that physicists, undeniably persons
with considerable inner life, also showed more *abstract*
movement responses, while psychologists showed more
human movement. This apparent parallel with the
Singer and Antrobus results is intriguing but no systematic link has yet been forged. Other explanations—
such as the association of verbal habit patterns to
motor activity—may more adequately explain the findings for the Rorschach M than does the drive theory
of Freud. Clearly, a great deal remains to be done.

Studies of the Drive-reducing
Character of Fantasy

Freud's conception that a fantasy uses smaller quantities of energy, thus partially reducing drive, has been

influential clinically in the development of the theory of catharsis so widely used in psychotherapy and particularly in play therapy with children. The work of David Levy who used dolls with easily detachable parts representing parents or siblings exemplifies Freud's conception. To the extent that a fantasy expression of hostility manifested in play reduces the aggressive drive (which a child dares not express openly), the symptom which is the outcome of a conflict will be alleviated. No self-respecting child guidance clinic today is without such dolls or comparable family toys, as well as punching bags and the popular prize-winning Bobo, a weighted giant balloon who bounces up again and again as children punch him.

I cannot avoid interpolating at this point a true story growing out of the use of the catharsis notion in therapy. A student therapist I was supervising reported that his eight-year-old patient had spent hour after hour the previous week pounding away at Bobo and saying, "Take that, Mrs. Jones!" (Mrs. Jones was his teacher.) The following week he repeated this but kept saying, "Take that, Mrs. White!" On being asked about the switch he simply said, "Oh, she's my new teacher. Mrs. Jones dropped dead of a heart attack." Suddenly my student and I had images of voodoo rituals which child therapists all over America were fostering in the name of the catharsis theory.

One attraction of the drive-reduction theory of fantasy has been its apparent ready translation into learning-theory terms. To the extent that the child engages in a fantasied gratification which shortly afterward occurs in reality, the possibility exists that this fantasy may take on the properties of a secondary reinforcer. This conception of daydreaming has never been extensively studied experimentally, but beginning with the work of Feshbach (1955) a series of experiments has sought to examine whether the strength of an induced drive, usually aggression, can be reduced at least partially by some form of fantasy expression.

Feshbach studied a group of students who were aroused to anger after being insulted by an experimenter who thereupon left the room. Half of the insulted group were given an opportunity to write TAT stories, while half were assigned a task which presumably precluded opportunity for fantasy expression of their anger. Feshbach found that the anger of those given an opportunity to engage in fantasy through story-writing was considerably less than that of those insulted students who had had no such opportunity. A control noninsulted group who also took the TAT showed less aggression on the ratings than either of the insulted groups, thus supporting the notion that fantasy was indeed partially drive-reducing.

Since all Feshbach's tasks involved verbal expression and not actual daydreaming, he was demonstrating that having written something in anger once, one has little further need to write it again. Had the subjects been merely asked to "think" of a story rather than write it, they might not have shown the reduction in aggression on the rating procedure. The use of thought, while admittedly harder to control experimentally, might have come closer to actual situations in which aggressive daydreams occur—for example, the fantasies of vengeance on leaving the boss's office after a dressing-down.

Two issues of interest grow out of the problem raised by Feshbach. One will be touched on only briefly since it focuses mainly on the interpretation of the Thematic Apperception Test. To the extent that fantasy is drive-reducing or cathartic, the person who tells many TAT stories around a common theme—for example, aggression, achievement, or sex—might be expressing a need in this area but might presumably be less likely to express this need in overt behavior. A contrast has been drawn between two issues in TAT interpretation—the "response-expression" and "alternative channels" hypotheses. The former suggests that an area of concern that occurs with high frequency in fantasy productions will also be likely to manifest itself in overt behavior, while the "alternate channels" notion predicts that behavior expressed in fantasy will be less likely to be expressed overtly (Broverman, Jordan, and Phillips, 1960).

The bulk of evidence in studies by Kagan (1956) and many others, as summarized by Buss (1961), suggests that fantasy expression of a need does not preclude its expression overtly and that strong emphasis on aggression in fantasy storytelling is indeed associated with overt aggressive behavior for the most part. The work of McClelland, Atkinson, and their collaborators in the study of achievement motivation (Atkinson, 1958; McClelland *et al.*, 1953; McClelland, 1961), has represented a careful and extensive demonstration of the high predictability of actual achievement striving when the achievement motive is scored through storytelling and related fantasy media. The work of Leiman and Epstein (1961) and Epstein (1962) has suggested that more complex factors such as fantasy-guilt expression and ego strength need to be considered in assessing the relative overt expression of thematic fantasy materials. Similarly, Brenner (1960), in a study carried out as part of our own daydream project, had adolescents rated by their peers for degree of overt aggression. Those who showed great anxiety (as measured by the Psychasthenia Scale of the Minnesota Multiphasic Personality Inventory) tended to reveal a greater discrepancy between their TAT expression of aggression and the overt expression, while those showing only moderate or "normal" anxiety were more consistent in their pattern, with little discrepancy between fantasy expression and overt behavior.

Part of the controversy over the alternate-channel versus direct-expression theories may be artifactual. It may well be that these studies, by focusing on the expression or failure of expression of a specific motive or need, are not taking into account the general meaning of fantasy in the response repertory of the individual. For someone who has an extensive fantasy life, engaging in a wide variety of daydreams of achievement or aggression may indeed be an available channel for these drives; yet this need not preclude their direct expression. Indeed, the fantasy rehearsal may lead to a more differentiated awareness of the appropriate situations for such expression. The person who lacks a capacity for inner experience—for example, the person who might score high on the items describing the extroversion factor in the Singer and Antrobus (1963) study—when aroused to anger or desperate need might have less recourse to fantasy at all and plunge directly into action.

Let us next consider some of the offshoots of Feshbach's work in a more directly experimental realm. Estess (1960), for example, found that fifth-grade boys, frustrated to anger after being given difficult arithmetic problems, showed less aggression following an opportunity to view an active cowboy movie. Saxton (1962), employing mentally retarded adults as subjects, also found support for the drive-reduction theory. He did, however, note that anxiety did not seem to be subject to this effect in the way aggression was.

A more direct attempt to study the effects of day-dreaming on an aroused affective state was attempted by Singer and Rowe (1962). In this case, it was of interest to ascertain the relationship of daydreaming to overt anxiety. Three classes of summer-school students received anxiety questionnaires as well as a daydream questionnaire at the beginning of the semester. A number of weeks later the students were suddenly confronted with a surprise midterm examination in their courses—this despite announcements at the outset of the semester that no midterm tests would be administered. Immediately after papers were collected, half the students had an opportunity to engage in daydreaming while half were given a task which to some extent precluded such activity. The general-anxiety and test-anxiety scales, as well as rating scales similar to Feshbach's, were then administered.

Those persons who had had an opportunity to daydream following the experimentally induced stress showed *more* test-anxiety but *less* aggression than their classmates who had not been given time for such thought. The results thus suggest a more complex situation than one merely of drive reduction. Fantasy may influence affective reactions differentially, increasing or relieving them in terms of the specific situation and affect. In this case it may well be that the persons who vented aggressive thoughts on the instructor had less need for continued expression of this feeling. At the same time, no amount of fantasy could relieve them of anxiety about a test for which they felt ill-prepared and whose outcome would not be known for some time. Indeed, the class that had been given an essay exam, in which students had the least basis for knowing outcome, showed the greatest increase in test anxiety after daydreaming.

A subsequent study by Rowe (1963) in the daydream project included physiological variables of stress. In this case, each subject was wired to an elaborate panel. Earphones provided subjects with instructions and limited external stimulation. The mere strangeness of the situation was reflected in striking increases in stress reactions as measured by elevated heart rate and galvanic skin reflex. Under the experimental conditions, the participants also heard an announcement that they would soon be recipients of electric shocks for experimental purposes. One group was then permitted, while awaiting this shock, to engage in thought or daydreaming, while the other group was assigned a digit-repetition task which, while simple, absorbed their attention and prevented extensive daydreaming. Nonstress, base reactions were also obtained. No shock was actually administered to the waiting subjects, however.

The General Daydreaming Scale (Singer and Antrobus, 1963) was associated significantly with a lower general level of heart rate prior to stress. During stress itself, those persons who had the opportunity to daydream showed less elevation of heart rate than did those who had no such opportunity. Thus, Rowe found some evidence that general fantasy disposition and the opportunity for daydreaming during a stressful period were associated with less build-up of physiological reactions.

A most valuable recent investigation by Pytkowicz (1963) has provided additional evidence clarifying the role of fantasy in catharsis. This investigation combined Feshbach's and Singer and Rowe's designs by using both TAT stories *and* free daydreaming as intervening tasks following prior induction of anger. The results indicated that *only for those persons who showed a predisposition to frequent daydreaming* (on the General Daydreaming Scale) was there a reduction in aggression following fantasy activity (TAT or daydreaming). In addition, and contrary to a simple energy concept of catharsis, the opportunity to engage in fantasy did not lead to a quantitative reduction in evidence of anger but rather shifted the emphasis from rage projected towards the experimenter to increased self-ratings of hostility. Furthermore, the high daydreamers who showed the reduction in direct anger did not resort in the intervening period to specifically aggressive fantasies but showed a more general range of daydreams, again contradicting a specific drive-reduction conception.

From the evidence cited it would appear that the notion of an energy system in which fantasy represents a partial drive reduction appears overly simple. A more likely interpretation may be derived from the theory of affects developed by Tomkins (1962) which we shall discuss in more detail in Chapter 6. Briefly, however, Tomkins has suggested that affects or emotions have certain innate activation patterns. Distress, for example, is activated by a prolonged moderate level of density of neural firing while anger is the consequence of a prolonged higher level of intense

stimulation. To the extent that daydreaming can temporarily provide another stimulus situation for the individual that is less negative and intense, it may relieve
some of the prolonged quality of the incoming stimulation and lead to a lowered level of neural firing. This
breakup of the pattern might not be wholly successful, but, if Tomkins's notion is correct, daydreaming
would relieve anger sooner than it would relieve distress; in other words, by reducing the general level of
stress from an intense to a moderate level, daydreaming would establish conditions for the experience of
distress emotions rather than anger. This theory can
explain the generally positive results for the reduction
of anger following fantasy but the failure of daydreams to reduce test anxiety. In Rowe's study
(1963), the moderate elevation of physiological stress
was itself lowered when individuals by daydreaming
could temporarily provide pleasant stimulation or
could at least distract themselves from thoughts about
the imminent shock; but the group with the enforced
continued level of attention was limited chiefly to
thoughts anticipating shock while concentrating on
the digit repetition. For persons who were skilled
daydreamers (in Pytkowicz's 1963 study), the opportunity to daydream also afforded them a chance for
relief from negative affect and changed their mood
somewhat. This is speculation, of course, and will be
discussed further in Chapter 6. It is likely, however,
that the notion of a drive as an internally originated
quantum of energy, which is the way it is essentially
presented in the psychoanalytic theory, is too narrow
a conception to deal with the complex aspects of the
relation of daydreaming to stress and affect.

The importance of the environmental stimulation

pattern must not be ignored, nor should the fact that daydreaming may itself create a new environment or stimulus field which feeds back alternative possibilities of response. Moore, in an unpublished study as part of the daydream project, found that hungry individuals who engaged in fantasy eating or in an assigned fantasy pantomime irrelevant to hunger, experienced time as passing *more rapidly* than did hungry subjects whose attention was absorbed by *nonfantasy* tasks relevant and irrelevant to the hunger drive. The opportunity to engage in some diverting fantasy play seemed to relieve stress so that time did not appear to drag during waiting. Obviously, considerably more work on relations of fantasy thought to time experience and drive and affective states is called for.

Drive-reduction and Drive-enhancement Effects of Fantasy Media

The focus of the present volume is, of course, on the actual daydreaming experience itself. Some comment, however, must be made on the effects of externally provided forms of fantasy, such as movies, cartoons, and TV. The issue raised has practical as well as theoretical significance. If fantasy or daydreaming, whether internal or provided through the medium of the TV screen, has the properties of reducing aggressive drive, then we need not be so concerned about violence presented to children in these media. Indeed, it could be argued that the great emphasis on military combat situations, spraying machine gun bullets of gangsters, barroom fights, or gun duels in cowboy movies, or the Japanese samurai movies, all represent adaptive devices by which society drains off excessive aggression and maintains some degree of stability. Thus the patterns of fantasy which characterize a society or the play or entertainments it devises may serve adaptive purposes.

On the other hand, one might just as well argue that perceived violence provides a feedback effect stimulating imitation and increasing the probabilities that a person once aroused to anger might be driven to open aggression under certain circumstances. Children who are angered and then exposed to an aggressive model in a TV movie might incorporate the aggressive pattern they have just observed into their as yet limited response repertory. They might then imitate such aggression directly at the first opportunity.

A stimulating paper by Berkowitz (1964) has clarified a number of issues in this controversy. Berkowitz carried out a series of experiments on the effects of observing aggressive behavior. In one experiment, angered subjects witnessed a violent movie about boxing. Under one condition Kirk Douglas was portrayed as receiving a much justified beating, and in the second condition he was described as about to strive for a better life. After viewing the films, the subjects were involved in a circumstance where they could administer electric shocks to persons who had insulted them. Those subjects who had witnessed the "justified fantasy aggression" administered much more severe shocks than those who had perceived the violence in the film as unjustified. Here was clear evidence that a fantasy medium could increase aggressive drive strength.

Other experiments cited by Berkowitz tend to support the conception that filmed violence can stimulate aggression. Walters, for example, found that hospital attendants who witnessed a movie involving a knife fight and who subsequently were allowed to administer "justified" shocks dealt more severe "punishment" than did a control group who had seen a nonviolent film. Bandura, Ross, and Ross (1963) found that children who observed an adult carrying out violent behavior in a playroom subsequently closely imitated this behavior when they themselves were aroused to anger and put in a similar situation. There were no great differences in imitation even when the model was perceived on film or disguised as a cartoon character. Mussen and Rutherford (1961) also found that children exposed to aggressive and neutral animated cartoons did reveal subsequent differences in aggressive attitudes; those who had seen the aggressive film were more disposed, if given an opportunity, to pop a balloon.

Suggestions for Further Research

Where does all this leave the theory of catharsis or the drive-reducing character of fantasy? It seems more and more untenable to view motivation as occurring on the basis of an inner drive such as aggression which has a specified quantum of energy that can be partially or fully discharged under various circumstances. Instead, it may be more useful to look at specific patterns of stimulus situations and of affective states. A cowboy movie might indeed, as Estess (1960) found, reduce aggressiveness after frustration in boys. This change may have occurred not because an aroused aggressive drive was partially reduced, but rather be-

cause a persisting frustrating situation which (in terms
of Tomkins's theory) would maintain a high density
of stimulation and irritability had been altered to a
pleasurable one by the movie itself. We need more
research evidence to show that the "control" movies
are as enjoyable as "aggressive" movies. To the extent
that an aroused affect is ameliorated by a change in
mood, we need not consider the drive-reduction
theory as the best approach to the issue of the adaptive role of fantasy. The same point can be made for
studies not of externally produced fantasies but for
actual daydreams. To the extent that the daydreamer,
by having an internal "laugh" over the revenge he
imagines toward someone who has put him into an
emotionally aroused state, can reduce the overall density of stimulation, the less likely he is to continue to
be angry. His anger might be reduced, however, not
only by specific fantasies of aggression, but also by
thoughts of escape, power, or success, which he finds
pleasurable. Specific studies along this line are much
needed.

One might also extend this issue to the problem of
other affects—anxiety or despair—which seem less
likely to be altered, or to pleasurable states. It may
well be that requiring persons to produce specific fantasies might arouse motivation in certain areas where
none had been in evidence (for example, sexual fantasies) or might lead to unpleasant moods or anger
(where fantasies of destruction were required to be
produced). Freeing oneself from the specificity of a
drive theory, as Tomkins (1962) has urged, prepares
the way for a more complex set of possibilities in
human behavior.

A factor not cited in most of the studies of drive

reduction, catharsis, or modeling, is the *meaning* of fantasy in the response repertoire of the child or adult. Children who emerge from cowboy movies or Tarzan on Saturday afternoons and run about almost at once in imitation of what they have seen generally recognize that they are playing a game. For the child who is used to playing fantasy games, the distinction between reality and fantasy may actually be more accurate than for the child who has little practice in fantasy. It is the latter child who may directly emulate the movie model and strike another child. In other words, to the extent that a person has a well-differentiated realm he considers play or fantasy, in which he can get pleasure or reduce a consistently high level of neural stimulation so that joy or other positive affects can intrude, the less likely he is to manifest anger in a socially direct fashion. At least he has the option of a varied pattern of behavior. For the child who has no such option, the combination of an aroused anger and the recent memory of an aggressive model may stimulate direct aggression.

A similar research question arises in connection with adults. We need considerably more evidence on the degree to which a person has trained himself to use fantasy as a means of changing his mood or expressing anger. Do experimentally aroused affects yield differential results for persons who have a fantasy option as Pytkowicz's data (1963) suggest? It seems clear that further experimentation must pay special attention to the long-standing predisposition of the individual, as well as to the situational variables.

Chapter

5

EXPERIMENTAL STUDIES OF ATTENTION AND THE PRODUCTION AND SUPPRESSION OF THOUGHT

In turning next to consider daydreaming as an *ongoing* process, we are confronted with new challenges. Can we find methods for studying more precisely the continuing patterns of relative attention to thought or fantasy without relying on memories or communication styles as we do in questionnaires? This chapter includes some new experimental approaches to these issues in the hope that they can serve as a basis for stimulating others towards more precise analyses and experimental study of the questions raised.

The Interaction of Environmental and Internal Sources of Stimulation

The important series of studies of the effects of sensory deprivation which were triggered by Hebb (1949) have, intriguingly enough, led to an increased awareness on the part of psychologists of the importance of fantasies and imagery (Holt, 1964). While studying the consequences for man of an environment in which stimulation is drastically reduced, investigators discovered that not only was such a condition exceedingly difficult to bear, but it produced an increased awareness of images and fantasies. Reports of hallucinations may have been exaggerated by the influence of some stimulus "leakage" (Holt, 1964); i.e., the failure of sensory deprivation conditions to work with complete effectiveness so that some stimulation from noise or light reached the subject. Another source of possible exaggeration may have been the fact that investigators reported hallucinatory experiences without efforts to study other inner experiences such as illusions, daydreams, or elaborate fantasies. Wexler, Mendelson, Leiderman, and Solomon (1958), who did attempt classification of a broad range of inner experience, found considerably more "daydreams, fantasies, and pseudosomatic delusions," for example, than hallucinations.

In effect, the studies demonstrate that when man is denied sources of stimulation from the outside, he either produces more inner stimulation or perforce *attends* more actively to the ever-present stream of imagery or fantasy. The *amount* of external stimulation itself may not be as much the problem as man's

need for *varied experience* (Fiske and Maddi, 1961).
Thus, when the environment is grossly limited in variety, one might expect an increased attentiveness to or
awareness of inner processes. This has often concerned persons in industry studying productivity or
accidents. A monotonous environment may be the occasion for shifts of attention away from the machinery to other stimulus sources, for example, badinage
with other workers, or to varied inner experiences
such as daydreams. Indeed, Wyatt and Fraser (1929)
long ago pointed out the extent to which daydreaming
might serve an adaptive purpose in maintaining arousal
during periods of monotonous work.

Let us assume, for the present, that we can desig-
nate two major channels of stimulation available to a
human being—the first, the external environment,
and the second, the inner dimension of his short-term
memories, elaborations of events perceived and events
from long-term memory storage, associations and
combinations of old memories with recently perceived
events or images just aroused. We may postulate that,
under most circumstances, response to external stimulus sources will have priority over response to inner
stimulation. When wide awake with eyes open, a man
will ordinarily be far more responsive to the changing pattern of external stimulation—the shouts of
children at play, a flickering of the light, the passing
roar of a train, the suddenly loud blare of a switched-
on television set, a fly on the wall—than to his own
inner associative stream.

Most normal behavior undoubtedly involves rapid
switching between the two channels; indeed, Tomkins
(1962) has proposed that consciousness itself requires
a rapid but not instantaneous matching of a perceived

stimulus with a centrally emitted image. As Korchin has noted (1964), man is typically capable of doing two things at once, of driving and talking, and, one might add, of driving and thinking. The ability to maintain both focal and peripheral attention processes or to switch rapidly between the two channels may well be a characteristic of an adaptive, alert person. Korchin has shown that a consequence of anxiety or stress is the restriction of the capacity to carry out two things at once. He writes: "To put it simply, the mature, well-integrated person can do two things simultaneously; with increased anxiety, one thing well (perhaps better); with still greater anxiety, nothing" (Korchin, 1964, p. 59).

The assumption that external stimulation has a higher priority, in general, over internal, may be a consequence either of the more insistent nature of sensory stimuli compared with those of memory, or it may be that most adaptive behavior requires a greater attention to the environment for survival. We do know that most persons report the greatest frequency of daydreaming as occurring just prior to sleep (Singer and McCraven, 1961). Under those circumstances, as one settles down for the night, consciously excluding varied external stimulation by shutting one's eyes and covering oneself with a blanket, there occurs an upsurge of awareness of inner activity. The increase of imagery and fantasy at this time may be so vivid and varied or effectively arousing as to maintain arousal even when sleep is much desired. Folk experience has suggested that this arousing effect of varied inner experience may be counteracted by sharply restricting the variety of inner activity. This is generally accomplished by techniques such as "counting sheep" which drastically reduce the variety of inner stimulation. Monotonous inner activity, coupled with the reduction in external stimulation at night, leads hopefully to lowered arousal and to sleep.

Let us consider some experiments studying effects of varied or monotonous inner experience during varied or monotonous external stimulus conditions. Antrobus (1963) and Antrobus and Singer (1964) investigated the effects of different degrees of inner and outer stimulation on a person's accuracy in monitoring a light signal. The situation was not unlike that of certain industrial automation or military radar situations where a man must monitor a repetitive signal and be alert for any changes in its pattern.

In the experiment developed by Antrobus (1963), the observer was seated in a small darkened and soundproofed booth. Before him was a small light that flickered intermittently, being on for one second and off for two seconds, continuously. The subject was required to press a hand switch whenever the light flashed just a little bit brighter than usual. The degree of extra brightness chosen was one that could be detected approximately 75 per cent of the time by the average observer. For every series of fifteen minutes of continued light presentation, six "signals" were randomly interspersed, to which the subject would have to respond by pressing his switch.

The observers were college students of about eighteen to nineteen. Following prior training trials they underwent a series of extended trials of one and one-half hours' duration each, called "main watches." During these sessions they were confined in a small booth, their physical motility sharply restricted. Their vision was limited to the observation of an inch-small square of light intermittently illuminated, and their auditory stimulation was limited to "white noise"—a steady hissing fed by earphones, which, while not essentially unpleasant, effectively prevented each from hearing his own voice.

Here, indeed, was a sharply restricted external environment with minimal distraction from the concentrated watching required. What of the "inner" environment? Antrobus sought to control this by studying individuals under two conditions—one when inner activity was varied, the other when the inner channel was extremely monotonous. Under the "varied talk" condition, subjects were required to maintain continuous free associative, spontaneous speech throughout the ninety-minute watch, while simultaneously attempting signal detection. Here they could attend to the ongoing varied stream of thought without restraint. Continuous "talk" was included as a check on compliance with instructions and their speech was recorded so that it could be related to detection scores. The alternate condition required the observers to limit their inner activity to counting from one to nine continuously for the ninety minutes. Here the subjects were permitted only minimal variety of inner activity. The "white noise" limited stimulation and auditory feedback and made the situation more analogous to thinking.

The results were indeed intriguing even though there were no overall differences in signal detection. Restriction of the inner environment led to a highly significant increase in drowsiness (measured by scales completed after each watch) and to instances of actual sleep during the watches. Arousal level appeared to be a function of the subjects' maintenance through free associative speech of a varied internal environment. This conclusion was clearly supported both by the scores of the Drowsiness scale and by measures of drowsiness even after the brief six-minute alert watches. Students also reported considerably more irritability and discomfort during counting and, in instances where they did not report actual sleeping, the tape of their speech, in conjunction with signal-detection records, supplied indications of varying periods of sleeping during the watch.

Why, then, did the greater drowsiness and greater number of instances of actual sleep not yield an overall advantage in detections for the varied-talk condition? A rather subtle analysis of the results suggested that when observers were awake and alert, the restriction of inner activity led to better signal detection than the varied inner activity. In other words, the monotonous talking task provided less competition and distraction during signal detection, but as time went on this lack of overall variety led to drowsiness and sleep. After a brief nap, the observer might well catch up on signal directions and surpass subjects who were allowed varied talk. One might guess that over an extremely long watch the varied-talk condition might prove more adaptive for signal detection by maintaining arousal, but that its interference with attention to the environment was also evident.

To check this point more carefully a second experiment was carried out (Antrobus and Singer, 1965). Here, to ascertain whether any negative (or interference) effect of varied talk could be demonstrated more directly, short, three-minute signal detection watches were employed. Thus, changes in arousal level would be minimal and changes in level could be maintained from one relatively short session to the next, with only brief interruptions. In order to insure wakefulness in the intervals between successive three-minute periods, lively march music played by a brass band was piped into the subjects' ears.

The results of this experiment indicated that individuals were indeed more alert during this study than they had been in the conditions of the previous investigation. With this overall increased alertness for both conditions, signal detection during varied talking was significantly inferior to that obtained during counting conditions. Here, then, was evidence that behavior analogous to daydreaming did indeed compete for "channel space" with the external task.

The results of the two studies suggest a logarithmic effect between varied stimulation (such as associative thought) and arousal. When a person is wide awake and alert, the varied spontaneous inner cognitive processes prove minimally effective in increasing interest, while when he is drowsy, these processes may have their maximum effect. Interference by attention to the varied inner channel may be more or less the same for all levels of wakefulness, however. When external sources succeed in maintaining alertness and a person can gain no advantage from the arousing effects of varied talk, the interference with detections by complex inner activity should be greatest. Since many kinds of industrial or mechanical operations are indeed what Broadbent (1963) has termed "understimulated tasks," the arousal effects of varied talk, or daydreaming, may, by maintaining wakefulness, mask their interfering effects.

A Simple Experimental Model

The reader may detect the beginnings of a small-scale theoretical model of the relations between fantasy and environmental stimulation. Let us assume that people can perform only a limited number of operations on either internal or external channels. As a person approaches this limit according to some pre-established priority system, he will selectively favor one channel over another. If we set up experiments which demand first priority for response to an environmental stimulus source, then, by varying the rate, complexity, or variety of such external sources, we can begin to study systematic variations in the rate of response to inner stimuli. In effect, if we make the demands for attention to the outside world great enough, we may be able to limit severely the individual's response to his own stream of thought.

Within the internal channel we can delimit two general classes of events. One set includes recent or short-term memory, that is, reactions to events that have occurred within seconds, while the other set includes events that vary greatly in relation to the whole life history of the person. To the extent that a task calls for either a direct response to an external stimulus, or a simple matching with an event occurring only seconds before (short-term memory), one might expect less likelihood of a person's noticing his own fantasies, images, or reminiscences which ultimately derive from relatively long-term memory storage. Similarly, we might classify these long-term memory events or other spontaneous cognitive processes and make some predictions about their relative order of disappearance as we increase demands on persons for response to external sources or to short-term memory. For example, we might propose that subvocal speech (termed verbal imagery) would be more vulnerable to disruption or disappearance than fleeting visual or auditory images which perhaps require less organized form and time for representation. A person required to react to a rapidly presented external stimulus might therefore report less awareness of a *monologue intérieur* during performance of the task than of rapid visual images.

By drastically reducing the variety and complexity of external stimulation, we may limit the responses of an individual either to the external task or to a variety of inner cognitive processes. Similarly, by limiting our inquiries to *task-irrelevant* thoughts or fantasies, we can approach more closely the "natural" stream of thought of the individual. It can be assumed that, following attention to any such thoughts, they too are stored, if only temporarily, in short-term memory. We can then, by prompt inquiry, obtain some useful information about such spontaneous cognitive processes before the subject has had sufficient opportunity to engage in defensive suppression or extensive secondary elaboration.

Let us now consider an experiment that demonstrates the use of this model (Antrobus and Singer, 1964). An individual is seated in a small, totally dark, soundproof room. He wears earphones which provide his chief source of external stimulation or communication with the experimenter. Following prior habituation and training to a desired level, he is required to monitor *auditory* signals. These consist of two pure tones differing only in frequency, one being pitched slightly higher than the other, which are presented continuously in a randomized sequence at controlled rates. These rates can be one per second or one tone every three seconds, but the same rate prevails for a given session of trials. One set of instructions, calling basically for a more direct response, requires the subject to press a switch when the tone presented is a low tone, or in an alternative group of trials, when the tone presented is a high one. Here, once training trials have established optimal discrimination, the task involves a relatively immediate response to each "beep" as it comes up. One need not recall what went before since the sequence is random, and all that is necessary is to press if the low tone is presented.

The second set of instructions involves short-term memory. The subject is to indicate whether the "beep" he hears is the *same as* or (in the alternate condition) *different from* the immediately preceding tone. He must therefore be constantly relying on immediate memory for successful performance of the task. In effect, we have moved a step "into" the organism, but presumably under conditions in which *task-irrelevant* imagery would be more of an interference. The speed of presentation of the tones can also be varied for all of these conditions.

The individual's task demands highest priority for response to an external stimulus source, the continued tone presentation. Other external stimuli are grossly reduced or masked and so cannot be responded to as alternatives. The subject can, however, engage in spontaneous inner activity which is irrelevant to the experiment, such as daydreams or memories. In this experiment the subjects were interrupted at irregular but predetermined intervals and required at once to

rate the frequency or magnitude of such task-irrelevant thoughts on special scales. These included categories such as verbal thinking, auditory imagery,
visual imagery, and kinesthetic imagery. A verbal account of task-irrelevant thoughts was also obtained
immediately following ratings. A subject in a darkened booth, attending to the business of listening to
tones, might find himself thinking of a recent date
with his girl, or planning a fraternity party, or imagining some relatively unlikely occurrence such as winning a great sum of money. Upon interruption, he
rated the relative frequency of such irrelevant
thoughts during this interval, quickly classified them
as to category, and described them. All this was done
out loud in response to auditory presentations through
earphones and taped so that delay, change of environment, or other distractions were held to a minimum.

The results of the experiment clearly indicated that
increasing the rate of signal presentation did indeed
reduce the number of reported task-irrelevant spontaneous cognitive responses. Similarly, demanding of
someone that he rely on short-term memory had an
even greater effect in reducing internal activity. The
most striking indications were that visual imagery and
task-irrelevant thinking generally were particularly
affected by changes in rate or by introduction of the
memory task. There was some evidence that verbal
imagery might have been greatest under the slow rate,
supporting the notion that it was abolished relatively
early as priorities for attention to external stimulation
increased. Although both visual imagery and task-
irrelevant thought were affected by both memory and
rate, there were clear individual differences in the
degree to which patterns of inner activity were altered

by the rate or by the memory task. It should be noted that the number of actual correct detections (which was 92 per cent) did not relate to the effects of the memory or rate conditions. The data also yielded evidence that (as found by Antrobus and Singer, 1964) *drowsiness* was accompanied by an increase in task-irrelevant thinking and visual imagery.

From this experiment it is thus clear that a carefully planned set of external demands can sharply reduce a subject's response to or awareness of internal spontaneous cognitive processes. At the same time, one of the most dramatic findings of the experiment was the magnitude of fantasies, daydreams, or reminiscences which were reported. It is indeed remarkable that a person can listen to tones presented at the rate of one per second, judge whether each is the same or different from the pitch of a preceding signal, indicate his judgment on a hand switch, while at the same time storing the just-rated signal for comparison with the one about to come (all with almost perfect accuracy) —and at the same time imagine a summer holiday or plan his next date with his girl friend. At least for the kind of subjects used in these experiments—college students—the motivation to engage in "processing internal events" is certainly very strong. Obviously it would take a much faster rate or much more complex task than was used in this experiment to abolish completely such daydreaming or imagery.

While the subjects in this last experiment did indeed show persisting fantasy behavior under increasing task demands, the likelihood exists that many persons would, if given a choice, give higher priority to externally oriented responses. In clinical literature this priority of perceptual response over fantasy, when it is a defense against self-awareness, is often termed a "flight into reality." And it is the relation of such perceptual responses (usually accompanied by eye movements) to thought and daydreams that we shall consider next in attempting to extend the model to problems of imagining and of suppressing thoughts.

Studies of Eye Movements During Daydreaming and Thought Suppression

An important methodological breakthrough of the past decade has been the work begun by Aserinsky and Kleitman (1953) and Dement and Kleitman (1957) demonstrating that the cyclical stages of sleep accompanied by periods of rapid conjugate eye movements (REMs) could be used effectively to study patterns of dreaming. The extensive work following these early studies has opened the way for a more systematic attack on man's inner experience, its relationship to his physiological and electrophysiological patterns, and its overall meaning for adaptive functioning.

Since the primary focus of the present volume is on daydreaming, no attempt will be made to summarize the nocturnal dreaming literature here. The major findings seem to be that, based on data from awakenings during EEG Stage 1 and associated REM periods, almost all persons so far studied show regular cyclical dreaming every night whether or not they ordinarily recall such dreaming. More refined definitions of dreaming (Foulkes, 1964) have brought out evidence that non-REM-period awakenings do elicit reports of thoughtlike content, so that it appears that REM-period content may represent a special phase of an ongoing stream of thought, more elaborate, vivid, and less logical. Some data suggest (with a number of methodological limitations) that the REMs observed through electro-oculargram measurement from dreaming subjects may be essentially visual tracking responses, the dreamer following the scene of his hallucinated image much as the waking observer manifests the saccadic eye movements of normal perception (Dement and Wolpert, 1958; Roffwarg, Dement, Muzio, and Fisher, 1962).

Can we extend these interesting findings to the study of the ongoing waking thought processes of an individual? How might we adapt some of the techniques of studying eye movement to the study of waking imagery and fantasy? The first step involved a phenomenological analysis of behavior during ongoing thought. Some of the questions that arose were:

1. Does it make a difference in eye-movement patterns whether eyes are open or closed during imagery?

2. Can we discern differences between ongoing dreamlike thoughts and direct observation, more formal thought, or rapidly shifting thought?

3. How do we stop thinking about something and suppress a daydream or change the subject mentally?

Observation of patients and other persons who were engaged in fantasy behavior as well as personal experience as a subject for an EEG exploration of ongoing thought led to some tentative notions and some formal experimental studies. The analysis of the possible relationship of eye movements to ongoing thought suggested that the simple tracking notion presented above in connection with dream studies might not be an adequate basis for interpreting ocular activity during ongoing waking thought. Let us examine the findings of an experiment and then attempt to relate these findings to the theoretical model of limited channels of stimulation and response, described in the previous section.

Antrobus, Antrobus, and Singer (1964), following some pilot studies, set up a formal investigation of ocular motility associated with ongoing waking thought. There were two general phases to the study: the first, a naturalistic examination of spontaneous thought (interruption technique), more like that used in dream research; and the second, a series of one-minute episodes in which persons were assigned specific thought content.

The subjects for this investigation were young college women. Each reclined on a bed in an otherwise bare and darkened room. There were some shadows, light changes, and street noises, and the rumble of a Fifth Avenue bus was audible. No attempt was made to eliminate such natural sounds or visual stimuli. Horizontal and vertical electrical oculargrams (EOGs) were recorded with standard electrode placements (Dement and Kleitman, 1957) above and to the side of the girls' eyes. The subjects were quickly able to habituate to the attached wires. During the first phase of the experiment, the young women were given no special instructions other than to keep their eyes open and to remain in bed. As time passed, whenever the EEG record met a criterion period of either continuous REM or of the same period of no REM, the EEG monitor signalled an interruption, and an interviewer who was unaware whether this was a REM or non-REM interruption proceeded to question the subject systematically about what she had been doing and thinking immediately prior to the interruption. The questions dealt with content of thought, degree of shift of attention, and visual activity either looking at objects in the room or at internally produced images. The answers were recorded on tape and rated by three judges who had no knowledge of experimental objectives or condition (eye movement or absence of eye movement) prior to interruption. Such controls are essential in a study of subtle inner processes.

During the second phase of the experiment, involving one-minute periods of thought along specified lines, in order to check whether tracking movements occur during waking imagery with eyes open or closed, the young women were asked to imagine scenes like "a man on a trampoline" (vertical) or "a tennis match" (horizontal). Static imagery was also called for, as well as "active busy thinking," "arithmetic progressions," and so on.

Of special interest were instructions during one episode to "engage in a daydream of the fulfillment of a secret wish, one you haven't told people." Subjects were encouraged to revel mentally in the fulfillment of this wish. A subsequent episode required subjects to engage again in this wishful fantasy but now to attempt actively to suppress it each time it came into consciousness—as if, in effect, they were blocking someone from reading their thoughts. This sequence, engaging in a wish-fulfilling fantasy and then actively attempting to suppress it, while eyes were open, seemed particularly relevant to the more natural condition of a person who drifts into a wishful dream and then, because of fears it arouses or its distracting quality, must actively suppress it. An analysis of the phenomenal characteristics of daydreaming and some pilot work led to the hypothesis that a person who was awake would show less eye movement during an elaborate daydream but more eye movement when attempting to break up a sequence of thought.

The results of these studies were on the whole quite clear-cut. During the spontaneous interruptions sequence the reports of content were judged as more "daydreamlike" by the raters when interruptions came after criterion periods of *no eye movement*. More active, objective thought was characterized by greater eye movement. *Internal* visual imagery was associated with minimal eye movement, while reported attention to external detail occurred in association with greater ocular motility.

The findings of the episodes phase of the experiment indicated that tracking eye movements did occur following instructed thought periods of an active type. These tracking motions were much more vigorous with eyes shut, however. Of particular interest were the significant results for the wish-fulfillment, wish-suppression contrast. The women showed very little eye movement while engaging in a daydream of their secret wish. In the suppression episodes, however, eye movements were extremely numerous.

A subsequent replication and extension of this work (Singer and Antrobus, 1965) sought to check whether the eye-movements contrast between imagine and suppress episodes would occur when eyes were covered as well as wide open (as they had been in the earlier study). Subjects were asked to imagine persons they liked, disliked, or towards whom they were neutral, and then to suppress the thoughts. Their heart rates were also recorded, in order to check on the possibility that the eye movements associated with suppression were a result of a general arousal state.

Again the findings indicated support for the hypothesis that eye movements were greater during suppression of thought than during active fantasy. The type of content did not seem to make much difference in this relationship but it might well be that more highly personal negative or positive fantasies could have been elicited with other instructions. The heart-rate data did not support the implication of a generally aroused state during suppression. Suppression was also characterized by eye movements under both eyes-covered and uncovered conditions, while daydreaming under those conditions showed little eye movement. An important methodological feature of these studies, in contrast with many night-dream investigations, is the opportunity to obtain statistical estimates of the subjects' consistency from episode to episode and of the degree of agreement between judges as important controls on potential bias in evaluating results.

The most interesting findings of these experiments are the absence of eye movement during daydreamlike thought and the indications that suppressing an on-going wishful thought pattern involves considerable rapid eye movement. These results are in contrast with findings for sleeping persons. A careful re-examination of the notion of tracking movement of the eyes during dreaming as a basis for the association of eye movements with dream reports seems desirable. In an important experiment Judith Antrobus (1963) found that women who were persistent nonrecallers of dreams actually showed *more* eye movements during sleep than did frequent recallers. The nonrecallers spent less time in Stage 1, REM-associated sleep, than did the recallers, but in that time their eye movements, and also small muscle movements, were significantly greater. It may be that, at least for these people, some eye movement and motor restlessness represented an effort to suppress or break up unacceptable fantasies.

Some Theoretical Considerations

Let us extend the "limited channels" model to the problem of ocular motility. It may be assumed that for a majority of persons, thought represents an internalized form of looking or listening behavior in which overt responses formerly associated with orientation and interest-affect are miniaturized for effective storage (Tomkins, 1962). The saccadic eye movements that characterize normal visual response are gradually reduced to brief spurts of horizontal or vertical eye movement. Suppose a man's eyes are open when he recalls an internal image of some event or is recombining stored events in an effort at planning or wishful thought. Because of the greater impact of environmental stimulation, he may find it difficult to avoid a direct response to his environment. If, moreover, he envisions some active scene and manifests associated tracking movements of his open eyes, he exposes himself to increasingly varied and perhaps more demanding external stimulus sources. Sustaining internal imagery under these circumstances may well be difficult. Indeed this may account for the "paler" or more fleeting quality of fantasy or daydreaming by comparison with night-dream imagery.

Daydreaming or other complex thought with open eyes may therefore necessitate relative ocular fixation in an effort to maintain an internal channel priority. This fixation may involve going out of focus with respect to the visual environment, or may be related to the "blank stare" of the person lost in thought. Socially one often detects that another person is not listening to one's conversation by the peculiar fixity of the gaze even when a fading polite smile still lingers on the lips.

What, then, of the fact that eye movements during Stage 1 EEG patterns are associated with more frequent reports of dreaming? Since external stimulation in the visual modality is markedly reduced during sleep, there may be greater freedom for tracking eye movements since external stimuli cannot interfere. We may have developed different habit patterns for waking and sleeping states as a consequence. Even in sleep, however, the extensive neonate and animal evidence of rapid eye movements during EEG Stage 1 (Oswald, 1962) suggests that tracking movement is not a sufficient explanation for the occurrence of these eye movements. More likely, eye movements are a cyclical physiological pattern with which the hallucinatory-looking responses become associated, almost incidentally.

As for the way in which thoughts are suppressed, one might speculate that just as a person shuts or averts his eyes to avoid noxious visual stimulation, so the attempt to avoid unpleasant thoughts or to mentally "change the subject" involves miniature ocular avoidant responses. Such eye movements may function to change input either literally, by active looking around the room, or by rapidly shifting inner cognitive material. These rapid shifts may well have long ago been habituated to ocular motility once associated with surveying a range of stimuli or searching responses. Luborsky, Blinder, and Mackworth (1963) have found striking evidence of avoidant eye movements during perception of threatening stimuli.

Some persons who have developed an extensive capacity for fantasy may have correspondingly learned how to fixate their eyes and blot out external stimulation. This might be done so skillfully that internal channels show an unusually high priority despite distracting stimuli to which others are sensitive. A skilled daydreamer can carry on an elaborate fantasy while dogs bark, children scream, whistles blow, and lights flash. Many persons, by contrast, cannot engage in internal response unless absolute silence prevails and there is minimal visual distraction. For the person unaccustomed to attending to his own ongoing stream of thought, the obvious recourse is a rapid flight into looking around a room. If the external environment is limited he may escape by engaging in rapidly shifting thought or repetitive obsessional ritual. One form of suppression, the extroversive, may involve active visual or motor response. In the case of motor restlessness, the environment is obviously rapidly changed and there is also kinesthetic feedback from musculature. The more introversive approach may involve a rapid sorting of fleeting internal content, a pattern such as that which is reflected in the "psychaesthenic" daydream factor reported in the Singer and Antrobus (1963) study, where many vague passing images occur with little content or continuity.

Why do people forget unpleasant events, traumatic encounters, ego-dystonic acts or thoughts? Why do people forget dreams when evidence now suggests that some form of thought activity (Foulkes, 1962) is almost continuous during the night? The answer may be that perhaps a certain degree of additional attention is necessary to any environmental stimulus in order to permit its storage. Recent studies of short-term memory suggest that such a crucial time period is needed for storage. Tomkins (1962) has proposed that effective interpretation of incoming stimuli requires a matching process between a visual or auditory image and a centrally emitted image. This process, while rapid, does take time and requires some reverberatory activity in short-term memory of the new stimulus.

A person either by rapid and continued motor activity or by rapid shifts of internal cognitive material may effectively prevent the sustained attention or central-image matching and interpretation that is necessary for permanent storage of stimuli. The same technique, effective in blocking out recall of external events, may also operate for internally produced cognitive events. We have all had the experience of having a sudden, original combination of associations yield a potentially creative solution, whether to an unimportant puzzle or a serious problem, and then, because we are suddenly distracted by noises or conversation, of being unable to recapture the idea because we did not have sufficient time for reverberation and sustained attention. Of course, if an idea has many associative connections because one has been gradually approaching a solution, then it may recur again, seemingly as a new idea. Often, however, very good notions are permanently lost in this fashion—a reason why most experienced writers, journalists, or scientists rely extensively on notebooks.

Even stored material must be revived into consciousness and rehearsed for its continued storage. The person who sustains attention to internal channels or who switches effectively between channels may engage in considerably more rehearsal activity of a variety of associations and images, thus increasing likelihood of their continued storage. On the other hand, someone who scores high on the extrovert factor in the Singer and Antrobus (1963) study, forever seeking out external stimulation or motor activity, may store less material in general.

Recent studies of cognitive styles—patterns of recurrent orientation toward cognitive experience—are related to this view of suppression and repression. For example, the hysterical represser personality has long been associated with an extroverted orientation in social response. The more concrete and unelaborated imagery of the hysteric described by Sullivan (1953a), and the hysteric's lower general information level noted by Rapaport *et al.* (1946), may reflect not an active forgetting process so much as a failure of registration or storage because of the extensive looking, listening, and rapid motility patterns as well as the failure to rehearse internal cognitive material in new combinations. The many attempts in clinical work to have such a person recall a past event may be doomed to failure because such events were not stored originally or were not reminisced.

Nonrecallers of dreams (Schonbar, 1959; Tart, 1962) and of daydreams (Singer and Schonbar, 1961) also reveal high scores on repression scales. As Rorschach long ago noted, dreams are best recalled if one lies quietly upon awakening and reviews the content with eyes still shut. Schachtel (1959) in his theory of memory carries this observation further and notes, in referring to forgetting of dreams: "This process . . . bears no relation to specific dream content. Therefore it seems to stem from the incompatibility of the ex-

troversive attitude of waking with the introversive attitude of dreaming rather than from resistance to specific strivings which are expressed in the dream
thoughts. The antagonism between motor activity and
dream recall brings to mind Proust's words that he
could recapture his former being only '*dehors de
l'action, de la jouissance immédiate*' and that in such a
moment he did not dare budge lest he lose the refound
memory of the past" (Schachtel, 1959, p. 307).

One may apply the same reasoning to the recall of
or attention to ongoing inner experience and fantasies
as well. If Antrobus's (1962) evidence of greater motor
restlessness and more numerous REMs during dream
periods for nonrecallers can be replicated, one might
also look for means of extending such a notion to persons who report relatively little daydreaming or general awareness of inner experience. Indeed, the possibility of an extended series of careful studies of the
relationship between external and internal stimulus
channel priorities and eye movements, motor restlessness, and so on, seems an intriguing next step after the
general model presented here.

Suggestions for Further Research

Extension of the miniature theoretical model and its
experimental outgrowths may open the way for further significant research. The work described above
has been done with students, who probably have a
greater priority for inner channel responsiveness *as a
group*. The use of late adolescents in whom fantasy
activity is in itself at a peak (Singer and McCraven,

1961) may influence these findings. The following are some other technical problems.

1. To what extent do findings about auditory detection apply to a visual detection situation? It may well be that given a visual task of some difficulty the demands upon visual response will be sufficiently great to eliminate visual imagery, which, as was shown by Antrobus and Singer (1964), comprises a good share of the task-irrelevant thinking variance. At the same time one might also examine the relative priorities of various modalities both as external stimulus sources or as imagery patterns. Or suppose the entire signal detection situation is translated into a game with subjects play-acting in fantasy a situation in which each signal detected is an enemy plane with the observer a radar man on duty in combat. Such fantasy alterations might provide enough variety to sustain interest-affect and motivation—to use Tomkins's (1963) terminology— and prove even more effective in maintaining both arousal and vigilance during an extended watch.

2. Individual differences in channel priorities during signal detection have not been explored in this model. Although McGrath (1963) did not report significant individual patterns in *detection* per se, the present model suggests that some persons may not sustain varied internal responsiveness as effectively as others and could become drowsy sooner. Antrobus (1963) found that persons who managed to sneak in some daydreaming while in the counting condition were less sleepy and more accurate in detections. Those persons who daydreamed *in addition* to the varied talk showed a drop in detections. This suggests that an optimal pattern of internal responsiveness without loss of abil-

ity to attend to an external channel may exist or that
individuals may differ markedly in their switching
capacities. Certainly it would be of interest to study
personalities already delineated as "levelers-sharpen-
ers" (Gardner *et al.*, 1959), "field-dependent-inde-
pendent" (Witkin *et al.*, 1962), or selected from
scores on relevant daydream scales (Singer and Antrobus, 1963) in their performance during signal detection situations.

3. The auditory signal study model has many invit-
ing features for personality studies. Despite reductions
in internal response occasioned by increasing task difficulty, many persons still produce considerable fantasy.
Is there evidence of individual consistency in such
resistance to reducing internal content, or conversely,
for relative readiness to reduce such content? One
might carry out personality studies of contrasting
groups or examine the content of the persisting fantasy material, and analyze it in terms of concepts such
as level-sharpening tendency, affective qualities,
primary-secondary process manifestations, and so on.
Incidentally, the task-irrelevant thoughts obtained
from subjects on tapes so far suggest that this technique has unique possibilities for studying content and
structure of ongoing daydreaming. The frankness of
material produced has been impressive indeed; the
brief time intervals and the requirement that the subject focus on external signals limit opportunities for
defensiveness or rationalization.

4. Other research possibilities of a more experimental nature which may be mentioned include the
question of "fantasy deprivation." Dement (1960), in
a most provocative study, found some indications that
persons awakened systematically during Stage 1 EEG

and REM periods suffered from restlessness and excessive daydreaming. He suggested that some basic physiological restorative function was served by dreaming. One might set up experimental situations that effectively minimize internal activity by increasing the complexity or rate of the external task, providing a reward for increased external channel attention (for example, reducing noxious stimulation), and introducing considerable external distraction for an extended period. We might find that such "daydream or general thinking deprivation" would have some unpleasant effects, particularly on frequent daydreamers.

Chapter

6

TOWARD A THEORY
OF DAYDREAMING:
CHILDHOOD ORIGINS

Some Experimental Studies with Children

Before moving to a more speculative integration of the
experimental data and clinical evidence concerning
fantasy development, it may be appropriate to describe some findings from our own investigations with
children. The major emphasis in these studies was
toward an initial approach to the function of daydreaming in children and toward a study of the relations of fantasy play to background factors in the
child's experience. In one study of this group, for example, Lesser (1962) found that children who are
characterized as imaginative by Rorschach and Thematic Apperception Test criteria played most vigor-
ously and aggressively in a free play situation before
and after experimental frustration. They "bopped"
Bobo and shot off the "burp gun" more often than less
imaginative children. In the same study, given a choice

of expensive toys as a reward for a task, the more imaginative children chose toys requiring minimal motor activity and greater fantasy interpolation (for example, a fort with soldiers or a science kit), while the less imaginative group more often chose toys that involved physical activity for its own sake (for example, a baseball bat or basketball). In effect, then, the data suggest that vigorous motor play is not a suitable basis for distinguishing between children of differing degrees of imagination but that the more imaginative have the greater option or inclination to introduce "make-believe" elements into their activities.

Another study sought to obtain additional evidence of the correlates in children of a consistent disposition to include fantasy elements in their play. In this investigation (Singer, 1961), children ages six through nine were questioned in a structured interview about their play patterns, imaginary companions, and "pictures in their heads," and then were classified into high- and low-fantasy play groups.

All the children also underwent a series of other procedures. They were questioned in some detail about parental interaction and family background factors, were asked to do some doodling after being given a choice of one crayon to use (red, yellow, green, or blue) and to make up original stories which were subsequently rated for creativity, achievement, and other motivational themes. Of particular interest was the rocket ship game. Informed that experimenters were looking for spacemen of the future, the children were asked to sit quietly in chairs for as long as they possibly could. It should be noted that care was taken not to mislead the children into believing this was an actual selection procedure; they were merely given a notion of what kinds of conditions were necessary for space flight. They were told that sitting quietly simulated the relative isolation and cramped space conditions prevailing in space capsules. The children were permitted under the first delay condition to indicate when they could no longer sit in place. In the second condition they were asked to stay in place for their estimate of fifteen minutes. Data on both measures indicated a moderately high individual consistency in waiting ability.

The results were fairly clear-cut. High-fantasy children were able to sit longer in place than the children who showed little indication of daydreams or make-believe elements in their play. The high-fantasy group proved likely to turn the delay into a quasi-fantasy situation and through some slight motor activity or mouth noises made it clear that they were pretending an actual flight.

The two groups differed on other variables as well. High-fantasy children were rated as higher in creativity for their stories by independent judges who had no knowledge of experimental objectives. Similarly, in making crayon choices they showed a significant preference for blue and green, the so-called "cool" colors, whereas the low-fantasy children often chose red or yellow, the "warm" colors. Some literature has supported the notion that the "cool" end of the spectrum is more often associated with measures of control, intellectuality, and achievement-motivation (Colvin, 1953; Atkinson, 1958). When interview and test protocols were rated by a clinician unfamiliar with the objectives of the study, children in the low-fantasy group were significantly far more often classified as hysterical personalities, high-fantasy children as obsessional personalities.

Some interesting results emerged as well from questions about background factors. The high-fantasy group reported considerably more interaction along fantasy lines (storytelling, fantasy games) with parents and indicated particular preference for or more extended association with one parent. The low-fantasy group more often indicated a nondiscriminating attitude towards their parents and considerably less personal interaction. Children in the high-fantasy group also proved to be more often either the oldest or only child or to have fewer older siblings than the low-fantasy children.

In effect, then, the results of this investigation led to at least the tentative conclusion that greater parental contact, less involvement with siblings, and greater storytelling creativity characterize children who report that they engage in more fantasy play. The ability to engage in fantasy play served to enable these children to sustain themselves more effectively when circumstances called for a long period of delay or waiting. A much earlier study .(Riess, 1957) had also found that children with more imagination (Rorschach M responses) showed greater motor restraint during a waiting period.

An attempt to determine whether training children to play fantasy games might enhance their delaying ability foundered because of the technical difficulties of developing suitable controls (Singer and Chipman, 1961). Some results may be cited, however, since an effort was made to inquire more directly about daydreaming through a verbally administered form of the daydream questionnaire used with adults. A test and retest carried out several weeks apart with a sample of twenty-three children of ages seven through nine yielded a correlation of .83, suggesting a satisfactorily high degree of consistency in response to this instrument. The daydream score for this sample correlated significantly with the two measures of delay in the rocket ship test. In a subsequent study with a larger group, it was found that children who indicated a greater degree of daydreaming also provided more internal "entertainment" or stimulation for themselves during the waiting period, while children who showed less disposition to daydream were also the ones who made more direct perceptual responses and seemed to depend more heavily on what Piaget has called the "stimulus nutriment" of the environment.

An outgrowth of these studies was an investigation by Singer and Streiner (1965) of the imaginative behavior of congenitally blind children. In view of the strong visual component in most reports of daydreaming and imagination, it appears that blind children may be doubly handicapped. Not only are they shut off from direct visual perceptual contact with the world but a whole realm of visual imagery is not available to them. Lacking such environmental stimulus nutriment they may be less likely to practice a variety of make-believe situations. One might surmise that young children born blind would show less make-believe play than an otherwise comparable sighted group. Formal studies suggest that when blindness occurs before age six, visual imagery is unlikely to persist into later life. The dreams of the blind, although utilizing auditory and kinesthetic imagery, tend to be somewhat reality oriented, traceable to specific day-residues or material recently read, and generally involve less variety in main character or type of conflict (McCartney, 1913; Kimmins, 1923; Blank, 1958). While some clinical observers have attributed greater fantasy disposition to the blind (Rowley, 1922; Cutsforth, 1933; Deutsch, 1928), none of their studies included comparison with comparable sighted subjects; lacking such comparisons these investigators may have overevaluated data that the blind do indeed engage in fantasy behavior.

In the Singer and Streiner (1965) study, a structured interview was carried out with each child pertaining to the structure and the content of the child's play habits, daydreams, and night dreams. Degree and nature of parental contact were examined, as were favorite games, any imaginary playmates, thoughts before going to sleep, and interior monologues. An actual recurrent fantasy, a new story, and an actual recalled dream were elicited from each child. The rocket-ship-waiting situation was also employed. The interview content was transcribed from tape recordings and rated by judges who were unfamiliar with the sighted status of the subjects or with the separate sections of the protocol.

The results made clear that blind children do engage in daydreams, make-believe play, and night dreams. Yet quite significant differences were obtained for each of the variables—namely, imaginative play, storytelling creativity, and creativity of dream content. In effect, in all cases the content of the material presented by the sighted children was rated as more make-believe, imaginative, or creative. Sighted children were also able to give significantly more specific ex-

amples of fantasies and had considerably more recall
of dreams. In one respect only did the blind children
show a greater fantasy disposition. This was in their
more frequent reliance upon an *imaginary companion*,
almost invariably a sighted person more capable than
the blind child. In the waiting situation the long-standing habituation of the blind to remaining passive or
controlling their motility counteracted the results
found in the earlier studies with sighted children.

An examination of the content of the daydream and
night-dream material corroborated the general rating
idea. The blind children's daydream and night-dream
content was more concrete, more closely related to
immediate personal experiences, and somewhat more
dependent in orientation. The sighted children
brought in many more fantastic or impossible elements
and their stories were freer of reference to family or
to daily routine activities.

An example of the contrast emerges in the stories
told by two children of quite comparable age and
background. Both involved a trip to the airport. The
blind child's story focused on the little boy's reaction
to the plane, his having a nice trip, and enjoying going
places with his mother. The sighted child, however,
described an adventure in which the pilot was
knocked unconscious when the plane hit an airpocket
so that the parents had to fly the plane back to the
airport. The parents taught the children to fly and the
children became famous pilots in the war and shot
down many planes. They were rewarded by receiving
as gifts from the Air Force two personal jet planes.
The blind child's fantasy thus appears to be a more
direct reflection of recent experiences, while the daydream and dream content of the sighted child repre-

sents a more complex pattern of interwoven associations leading to a product that is more original or abstract.

While it is obvious that blind children, through reading Braille and listening to talking story-books, radio, and TV, can make up some of the imaginative decrement resulting from lack of visual imagery, nevertheless the overall gap remains large. "Blindisms" (repetitive rocking or eye-rubbing motions) and immersion in other concrete kinesthetic or auditory experiences may somewhat replace the visual and provide a degree of stimulus nutriment, but it is unlikely that such stimuli are as conducive to evoking fantasy patterns as visual stimuli are.

In general, the series of studies and observations as part of our general research program on daydreaming raise the question of the importance of varied environmental stimulation in forming the basis for fantasy development. The impression gained seems contrary to the classical psychoanalytic formulations which stress imagination as arising from instinctual sources that have been blocked from expression. It seems more likely that the child who engages in fantasy play is not necessarily withdrawing from "real" life or responding defensively to inner instinctual promptings. It may be more likely that he is actively exploring his environment visually and then continuing this exploration in play. Curiosity, pleasure in development of imaginative skill, and some defensiveness may all combine to foster fantasy play as a strong disposition in a given child.

Daydreaming as a Cognitive Skill

Let us now consider some of the significant implications of the body of research we have summarized so far in this volume. The position to be presented here represents both the fruits of personal investigation and thought and the opportunity to examine other positions which will be cited here.

The position to which I refer represents a somewhat groping effort to move beyond behaviorist reductionism which focuses too much on overt response and the psychoanalytic reductionism which (even with the development of ego psychology) overemphasizes drives and neglects the subtle interplay of external stimulation with ongoing inner states. Hebb's (1949, 1959) influential theoretical and experimental work must be acknowledged as one force that has opened the way for a deeper look both at the ongoing reverberatory activity of brain process and at the motivating properties of the environment in its complexity and unfamiliarity. White (1959, 1964) and Schachtel (1959), working somewhat more closely to psychoanalytic theory and clinical observation, have pointed out a position which stresses the importance of organismic development *for its own sake*, so to speak, rather than in the service of specific erotic or aggressive drives. In this respect their work also reflects some of the influence of the thought of Lois and Gardner Murphy, Piaget, and Werner. Quite recently Tomkins (1962, 1963) has also presented a point of view which emphasizes the great significance of affects or emotions as motivating properties of behavior and attempts to show the relation of affect to both the complex regulatory and feedback processes within the organism and to the density of neural stimulation provided by the complexity or novelty of environmental stimuli.

Within the framework of this "third force" in psychology—this cognitively oriented approach with its avoidance of drive-reduction theory—the phenomenon of daydreaming can be viewed as a more general capacity of the organism—a potential skill in Bartlett's (1958) sense—available for development in particular directions and under specific enhancing circumstances. The daydream is one manifestation of an ability to attend to internally produced stimuli or to use those stimuli to construct a new stimulus source less monotonous or less threatening than some external stimulus patterns.

If we assume that the brain is indeed continuously active, then the organism is constantly confronted with a competing source of stimulation from within. The feedback from the ongoing activity of the body itself must also be considered. At any given moment, just in sitting and other postures, there is stimulation of kinesthetic and tactual modalities. Smells and sounds from one's own body (for example, the gurglings of one's stomach) are all fed into central organizing areas of the brain and, in effect, compete with the reverberatory associational stream. The latter consists of recently perceived stimuli as well as associations from long-term storage which emerge either by linkage with recent stimulation or, very likely, almost randomly by the very nature of the activity of the brain. As Tomkins has put it: ". . . The central assembly is at best an untidy aggregate. It has none of the orderliness of our present-day [computer] programs.

It is perpetually vulnerable to interference, drift, dis-
assembly . . . it is more like an information stew than it
is like a program. . . . As nature is said to abhor a
vacuum, so psychologists have been loathe to look
entropy full in the face" (Tomkins, 1963, p. 41).

The important work of Witkin and his associates
(1962) suggests that long-standing differences in perceptual orientation may develop which represent important stylistic differences in perceptual and motor
priorities. Similar important stylistic differences in attention to internal or external stimulus channels may
develop which have unique value to a given individual
or turn out to be adaptive to very special environments. Barron (1955), for example, found that Rorschach M-perceivers were consistently rated as different personality types from persons who saw few
Rorschach M, but that these differences were not manifested in test performances and certain skills as much
as in the impression the M-perceivers made on others.
Similarly, one of the implications of the Singer and
Antrobus (1963) factor analysis of daydream scales is
that persons may differ strikingly in their style of response to inner experience without necessarily mani-
festing greater neurotic tendencies in one or the other
pattern.

In essence, then, it is argued that the relative reliance on priority assigned to various channels of stimulus information, grossly termed inner and outer, is an
individually developed skill pattern which may or may
not have long-run adaptive import. The person disposed to creating pleasurable stimulation by attention
to his own thoughts may well withdraw some attention from the external environment but he may have
also learned to make certain modifications in his be-

havior to manage this. The daydreamer may "see" less when he drives but he may have learned to drive more slowly in general than the person whose pleasure comes from his active involvement in the speed or physical experience of wind on the face, the flashing by of scenery, or his catching up to and passing another car.

As with any skill, the response to inner stimulation may be put to a variety of uses or serve purposes which are not always desirable. Daydreaming might well serve a defensive function, as originally noted by Freud, so that an individual could avoid awareness of sexual fears or doubts through fantasied prowess in semi-disguised form. As such a defensive reliance on fantasy persisted, the skill might be overvalued. Its once defensive utility no longer advantageous, daydreaming might persist as a withdrawal state or obsessional substitutive symptom. A patient in psychoanalysis impressed by a newly discovered ability to track down a sudden fear or affective response through examination of an associative chain may turn into a bore at parties or may use the technique to avoid confronting a more serious personality problem. Whatever the uses to which daydreaming may be put, however, it seems best regarded as a capacity available to most persons for assigning priorities to particular sets of spontaneous internally produced cognitive stimuli.

Tomkins (1962, 1963) has offered some cogent arguments for assigning to the less specific affect system a more important role in motivation than to the specific drives. He has also suggested that there are certain innate activities of the positive (surprise, interest, joy) and negative (rage, fear, distress) affects. Briefly, he has argued that negative affects are aroused by a persisting high level of density of neural firing which can be produced either by an unpleasant or unfamiliar external situation—or, I might add, by a series of internal associations or memories, for example, the details of the death of a loved one. A reduced density of neural firing produces laughter, smiling, and the experience of joy. Here the conception verges close on Freud's concept of drive reduction, but it is extended by Tomkins's emphasis on surprise and interest as positive affects activated by a gradual rise in stimulation. Thus the individual, in striving to maximize pleasurable affect, may seek and welcome new stimulation. To the extent that new stimulation can be produced by attention to inner ongoing reverberatory activity or by construction of new internal environments through organized daydreaming, the individual has available an additional dimension for achievement of positive affect.

Once a long-standing disposition has been developed for assigning a high priority to internal channels, however, there may not be any turning back. The internally sensitive person may have to confront not only pleasant, but unpleasant memories, not only familiar or welcome associations, but also awareness of doubts, fears, and hatreds. This may account for the generally significant correlations obtained between daydream frequency measures and various anxiety scales. The penalty of self-awareness and introspection is the direct confrontation of anxiety. The extrovert or represser may well experience the same degree of anxiety symptomatically or in the form of insomnia and somatic ailments. For many persons who have developed priority for internal channel response and who also have serious personality problems, self-awareness may take the form of repetitive anxious fantasies which maintain the high level of density of stimulation, creating despair and distress. Such negative fantasies may also be used as repetitive obsessional substitutions preventing attention to a more seriously disturbing psychological problem; for example, a persistent hypochondriacal fantasy may prevent awareness of sexual inadequacy or of irresponsibility and failure in a significant social obligation.

The Internalization of Play

THE FUNCTION OF FANTASY

It may be possible to understand the implications of the cognitive-skill approach to daydreaming if we begin by speculating somewhat as to its development in childhood. Piaget (1962), in forty years of careful observation of the development of thought and language in children, has been struck by the interaction of two general processes which he terms *accommodation* and *assimilation*. The child must on the one hand accommodate his perceptual and motor apparatus to the outside world—he must make appropriate differentiations of figures and grounds, of colors, of shapes, and also of the significance or utility of certain perceptual objects or of certain motor responses. This adaptation to the "real" world is, of course, limited by the actual inherent skills and maturation level of the child, and by (a factor rather neglected by Piaget) the particular interaction patterns established by parents. On the other hand, whatever is available from the outside world is assimilated in the cognitive and affective system which is already functioning for its own sake *within* the child. Thus the information which the out-side world makes available to the child becomes a part of the child's own internal sphere and plays perhaps quite a different role there than might be anticipated by the adults. This conception has been elaborated upon by Schachtel (1959), who has noted how material that is obvious to adults, for example, a story like "The Three Bears," takes on for a child quite a different significance in its own right and forms a much different associational pattern in the young child's memory storage system.

When we observe a young child imitating a sound or a gesture and we laugh in a positive way, he strives to repeat this act and to adapt his motor and per-ceptual apparatus to ours. Yet, when alone, he may repeat the word or gesture and begin to work it into a pattern that bears no discernible relationship to the adjustment he made for the sake of having contact with the adults. The inherent reward qualities attained by increasing emotional experiences of interest and joy lead the child when alone to attempt to use the material he has incorporated through his imitative ac-commodation to create new sources of change and pleasure. This assimilative process, free of any con-straints to reproduce exactly the external world, per-mits a freer combination of associations and accounts both for the bizarre and the creative quality we dis-cern in children's play. Later the child may take the fruits of what he has practiced for its own sake and bring these back again to some accommodation to the outside world. In this case, as Piaget notes, the com-bination of creative inner activity with an awareness of the demands of the outer world leads to effective thought or what Piaget calls "operations." But even in later life the continuation of assimilative activity plays an important role in developing creative thought, while accommodation results in careful recall or imitation of what is appropriate in a social circumstance.

The picture I have been striving to present is of an active, curious, almost endlessly inventive child, given, however, material from without, with which he can deal. For the very young infant little enough is needed, and his own body, his own movements, the appearance and disappearance of his own hands—all these can suffice. As he masters these simpler perceptual, motor, or imaginal integrations, he requires more complex material, and this must be provided in part by his parents. The reader familiar with the psychoanalytic model of development of thought presented by Rapaport (1951) (see Chapter 4, above) will sense that Rapaport's portrayal is of a passive, helpless infant in whom a hunger need arises, a hallucinatory image of the breast occurs, temporarily delaying distress over failure of gratification, gratification is available, and then activity subsides. By contrast, the emphasis here is upon a more actively curious child, who enjoys play for its own sake. As both White (1959) and Schachtel (1959) have pointed out, the child who is under great drive pressure is less likely to explore or play. Instead, observation suggests that the child's more creative learning occurs under states of relative biological satisfaction.

Although the internalization of spontaneous play into symbolism and the daydream is largely completed by early adolescence, it is undoubtedly a very gradual process that probably continues through life. Let us consider some of the conditions particularly conducive for an earlier, more extensive, and more differentiated skill in fantasy or daydreaming. We must begin by accepting the possibility of very real difference in constitutional predispositions in children. Some are more motorically active than others, some apparently more prone to anxiety under pressure of need; for some the build-up of what Tomkins calls density of neural stimulation is too rapid and its reduction too slow to permit easy smiling or joy. When an infant fails to respond with a ready smile, the onlooking parents' disappointment feeds back further distress to the child. This can create a dangerous circle of anxiety which allows only brief periods of reduced stress and emotions of joy or interest. Under such circumstances, spontaneous play or exploration may be much less than in other children and opportunities for fantasy development may be hindered. We may assume that, while man seems by natural selection uniquely capable of complex symbolism and imagery, such capacities are not uniform and internalization of play into imagination and a fluid associative stream may come more easily to some than to others.

The capacities for image formation and symbolization and for adopting an "attitude towards the possible," as Goldstein (1940) has put it, may well be a product of natural selection and are available for man's development. The growing child takes pleasure in his very use of these capacities—as White (1959) has argued in developing his notion of the sense of competence. At earliest stages this pleasure is evident in simple peek-a-boo games, in which the child is delighted by the rise and fall of tension in the "now it's here, now it isn't, now I can bring it back." The sense of efficacy which a child obtains from this capacity to hide or uncover his own hand or a rattle he is holding undoubtedly furthers his inclination to try other types of make-believe play. And, it may be noted, this capacity for control may be one step in the child's learning to differentiate between himself and his environment—"*I* can make my rattle go away and come back!"

The self-actualizing tendencies, the play for its own sake, the sense of efficacy that comes from realizing that one can have an effect upon the environment, undoubtedly develop into the capacities for symbolization, imagery, and as-if behavior. The child still has to learn how to exercise some of his make-believe skills. Here early individual differences may play an important role. I have observed children who show tendencies towards organized play well before the age of two and for whom the disruption of a line-up of toy cars or blocks is quite upsetting. These children play well alone and are no "trouble" to parents until put into social situations such as the playground of an apartment house or nursery school. There, the more kaleidoscopic play patterns of other children who cannot sustain the game or continue the line of toys or blocks lead to great distress for the child who tends towards "organized" play.

THE INTERNALIZATION PROCESS

At first, lacking sufficient perceptual differentiation, the child is content to use sticks for guns and blocks for cars, just as he may continue for some time to be undifferentiated in his verbal patterns. But as perceptual differentiation increases, the child may not be as satisfied with using any stick as a gun and any block as an airplane. His urge to play is great and he will make do, particularly if he has already shown some skill at make-believe. There is no question, however,

that beyond the preschool age, the excitement of having more realistic-appearing toys is very great.
Whether such realistic toys impede further fantasy
development is an intriguing question.

As the child plays during the preschool period he
combines considerable overt motor activity, running
around, jumping, galloping like a horse, with much
verbal expressiveness. Some verbalization involves imitation of sounds, for example, the engine-roar of a
plane, or the narrative description of his game in the
telegraphic, limited vocabulary of so young a child.
One thinks of Piaget's (1932) charming description of
the egocentric speech of nursery school children at
play, in which two children, side-by-side, verbalize at
length about their individual games without, however,
really attempting to communicate.

At a later age, verbalization may be more elaborate and motor play more differentiated, reflecting
increased sophistication and environmental imitation
and differentiation. Erikson (1963) has employed a
delightful excerpt from *Tom Sawyer* to exemplify the
play of the nine- or ten-year-old. As Tom paints the
fence, along comes Ben Rogers munching an apple,
hop-skipping and jumping and engaging in a rather
elaborate verbal and motor imitation of the steamship
the *Big Missouri*, full of sound imitations, "Ting-a-
ling," "Chow-ow-ow," and barked orders, "Get out
that head-line! Lively now!"

Erikson goes on to say: "My clinical impression of
Ben Rogers is a most favorable one and this on all
three counts: organism, ego, and society. For he takes
care of the body by munching an apple, he simultaneously enjoys imaginary control over a number of
highly conflicting items (being a steamboat, and parts

thereof, as well as being the captain of said steamboat, and the crew obeying said captain); while he loses not a moment in sizing up social reality when, on navigating a corner, he sees Tom at work. By no means reacting as a steamboat would he knows immediately how to pretend sympathy though he undoubtedly finds his own freedom enhanced by Tom's predicament" (Erikson, 1963, p. 210).

It seems clear that gradually less and less play is verbalized or expressed in gross motor fashion. By the ages of ten to twelve, many boys still seem eager to continue such activity but it now takes a social form with as much equipment—toy guns, packs, helmets—as is feasible. Solitary play of this type is less often verbal, and drawing may be used as a vehicle. As the child continues to play but inhibits overt motor activity, he may gradually, if Werner's theory of sensory-tonic vicariousness is correct, be sensitizing his brain for apparent motion perception—one basis for the stuff of imagery. His drawings or his television-watching provide him with content which he partially enacts and then inhibits motorically. Similarly his verbalizations, which in preschool age were sketchy for lack of content and elaborate during the ages five through nine, as Ben Rogers's were, now again become telegraphic, so that observing the fantasy play of an older child one catches only whispers of sound imitation or conversation. What seems to be happening is that the child, no longer able for various reasons to re-create his game each time through elaborate motor activity and vocalization, is finding a means for storage of the associational content in a form readily available on demand but not requiring public manifestation.

What I am suggesting is that for the younger child

who can play publicly there is little need to store content from a previous day. Each fantasy game is *almost*
a new one, with the overt motor activity and verbalization presenting through feedback a new environment of interest to the child. Obviously some gradual
storage of content does occur, and phrases, sounds,
and motor content of the game come more readily to
the child with a bit of practice. But before social
pressure or ridicule forces inhibition of overt play,
any storage of previous play content is evident only in
the greater elaborateness of overt fantasy play. As
pressure for internalization increases, however, storage
becomes more essential. A fairly systematic, if perhaps
unwitting, effort is made by the child to transform his
motor and verbal reactions into a form available on
demand, without the elaborate overt feedback of self-
produced kinesthesia, sight, and sound.

Tomkins (1963) has provided the beginnings of a
theory of memory which may suggest how fantasy
play material can become stored as a series of images
or conversations available more or less on demand
without overt reconstruction. According to Tomkins's view, which makes use of computer terminology, the technique of storage of specific material involves ". . . a process of informational compression in
which the individual produces more and more miniaturized copies of the original information. This he
does by using the original to produce a more miniature copy, which in turn is miniaturized in a series
which in turn is miniaturized in a series. . . ." (Tomkins, 1963, p. 42).

This transformation of an overtly reproduced response, whether motor or verbal or quasi-perceptual,
by miniaturizing for storage seems to some extent

what may happen in the internalization of fantasy play. The child slowly and with many repetitions compresses the content of his play and verbal material. His motoric inhibition, following Werner's sensory-tonic theory, may lay a groundwork for a particularly movement-oriented perceptual sensitivity. At the same time he gradually compresses the content of his play, reducing it to miniature both by speeding up content into more and more telegraphic verbalization and more controlled motor patterns (for example, drawing as against overt movement) and by speaking more and more softly. The compression of the fantasy response into a miniature form probably takes years of effort. My experience in observation as yet suggests no clear hierarchy of order for the various modalities, although obviously the greater degree of motor activity is first to be internalized. A child between ten and twelve may show a little overt motor exemplification of fantasy play but one can still see him providing visual stimulation through drawings, and an occasional hushed "Bang-bang" or "5-4-3-2-1-blast off!" may leak out in public. One cannot avoid the thought that such compression not only miniaturizes specific components of fantasy play but also leads to compression of a whole pattern of approach to fantasy material or verbalization, so that there is increased tendency to transform conversation or visual content into comparable internalized form. Undoubtedly there are individual differences of great consequence in the sequence of miniaturization for modalities, in the systematic effort at miniaturization itself, and in the subsequent continuation of internalized fantasy play as a valued personality dimension. What has been described so far is the more general process which may reflect the way in which at least the minimal degree of internalization occurs for most children.

Let us next consider some of the more specific conditions which may strongly influence great individual differences in the internalization process and in the assignment of priorities to inner or outer channels.

The Role of Parental Interaction in Fantasy Play

RELIEF FROM NEED-PRESSURE

Although Piaget refers to imitation as a manifestation of accommodation and White makes much of effective environmental response and curiosity, neither investigator has commented to any extent on the interpersonal interactions which form a crucial part of the child's environment. The theoretical position of Sullivan (1953b), and what may loosely be called his school of thought, has forced upon psychology a much more careful consideration of the ways in which parental attitudes and patterns of parent-child interaction play a critical role in personality development. In relation specifically to child development and patterns of imitation and identification, the recent experimental work of Bandura and Walters (1963) has also called attention to the extensive influence of the parental model. As one might surmise from the earlier section on experimental work with children, there has as yet been relatively little formal study of parental influences on the development of daydreaming or inner experience. What follows, therefore, represents a speculative construction gleaned from hints in research findings, clinical observation, and the experience of being both a parent and a child.

As White (1959) and Schachtel (1959) have noted, the manifestations of exploratory or creative play are most likely to appear under conditions in which biological drives are reasonably well satisfied and anxiety kept to a minimal level. The early experience with a benign and effective parent who can anticipate the infant's and young child's needs and maintain a reasonably natural and consistent schedule of feeding, sleeping, cleansing, and social stimulation will prevent the excessive persistence of unpleasant affective experience. Under such benign circumstances the child will be freer to begin the exploration of its body, of its motor control, and of the environment that is essential for effective ego development as well as more specifically for the development of make-believe and "as-if" games. It is this active play and interest in seeking stimulation that leads the child to construct new environments or new play situations when the novelty of a given toy has been lost. Once a child has explored a set of blocks as blocks and has determined the properties of the set, such as what stands on what and how high the tower may go, the next step may be to convert the blocks into a city or a schoolhouse or army fort. This crucial next step towards the development of an "as-if" play pattern is most likely to occur when the child has enough *time* to explore thoroughly the more direct perceptual-motor aspects of his contact with blocks. If he is hungry or frightened, the recurrent awareness of the unpleasant affect amplifying the drive signal (as Tomkins puts it) might break up sustained attention to his blocks.

I do not mean to deny that children work out unresolved conflicts through play or to say that their play cannot manifest anxieties or sexual orientations.

Erikson (1963) has ably exemplified some of these manifestations through play of the problems of the child's world. What I am suggesting is that such uses of play to deal with fears of loss of love, sibling rivalry, or traumatic experiences can come only after the initial skill of as-if behavior has been developed to a reasonable level. The children who can "work out" or show signs of problems in their play are children who have already sufficiently learned how and had the opportunity to engage in make-believe. And such opportunity can come only if there has been at least some degree of parental attentiveness or consistent satisfaction of basic needs and affectional strivings. The children whose play is generally cited in case reports to exemplify evidence of conflict expression are usually middle-class children whose early basic needs were indeed cared for, even though particular areas of conflict with parents or siblings emerged later. It is quite likely that children whose early experiences involved greater direct frustration of biological need or who lacked a consistent and reasonably benign parental figure have never sufficiently mastered the art of as-if play or, later, the internalization of such play into daydreaming. Such children often are seen clinically as hyperactive, anti-social, impulse-ridden—the "acting-out" child so disruptive to the routine of the residential treatment center.

Although more systematic study is obviously rather urgent, some scanty evidence is available to support this view. Goldfarb's (1949) work with children reared in institutions during their very early years has yielded indications that they are in adolescence hyperactive, incapable of delay, and lacking in ability to rely on inner experiences, as evidenced by poor planning and lack of Rorschach M responses. Unpublished data obtained by Ralph Colvin at the Astor House for Children also have indicated that children institutionalized shortly after birth are more likely by ages nine through twelve to be rated high on impulsiveness and hyperactivity and lack of imagination than are otherwise comparable children who had even a few early years of some experience either with their own family or a foster family. A study by Singer and Sugarman (1955) indicated that schizophrenic patients who show more Rorschach M also present significantly fewer negative accounts of parental figures or indicate greater accessibility of parents in their TAT stories.

THE MOTHER'S ROLE

Thus far I have stressed perhaps the most essential features of parenthood in the early years—the maintenance of a benign atmosphere for early child development. But other important aspects of the parental role must be considered. The mother carries on a subtle affective interaction with the child as well as providing for its basic needs. Sullivan (1953b) has written with great sensitivity about how parental anxiety may be communicated to the child. More recently Tomkins (1962) has dealt in detail with the interplay of the smiling response between mother and child and its importance in establishing a basic communication system. In the pleasurable contacts which come with an interested (and interesting) mother, the child may be more likely to attempt an accommodating imitation of her sounds, her smiles, her movements.

Mowrer (1960) and Lair (1949) have dealt in detail with the role of a benign relationship between mother and child or even master and pet in eliciting imitative responses. Such stimulation is undoubtedly especially important in the learning of language and of culturally appropriate affective behavior. Its role in the development of fantasy play may come in the absence of the parent, when the child in its assimilative phase uses the motor and verbal responses of the parent in its own play by itself. The child's efforts may reflect an attempt not only to reinstate the absent parent (as Freud has implied) but probably to create through its own use of these gestures or sounds the positive affects experienced before with the parent.

The mother's role is not just one of familiarity, although regularity and frequency are of tremendous importance to a child to establish the degree of familiarity which adults attain with each other at a glance (Hebb, 1949; Schachtel, 1959). By saying funny things, by playing peek-a-boo games, by lightly bouncing the baby, the mother creates an *atmosphere* novel yet not startling, hence arousing the positive affect of interest (Tomkins, 1962). She creates an atmosphere of play itself as a means by which the child learns to obtain positive affective experience. For the child past infancy, the mother's play more clearly fosters the "as-if" attitude. Her singing and rudimentary storytelling, the use of games like "Where did the cereal go?" as a technique for getting the child to eat, all establish a stimulus complex which the child will attempt to imitate when the mother is present to elicit her smile (accommodation) and will engage in when alone to amuse itself (assimilation). Needless to say, mothers differ in the flexibility of their own behavior with the child, and the hungry, harried, anxious, or rejecting mother will herself be less capable of the playful exploration and creativity in the nurturing of

her child which is one of the greatest arts of feminin-
ity.

To some extent Western civilization and most of its
subcultural groups have left to the mother the role of
fostering language development, storytelling, and
inner experiences such as religion. Goethe, for instance, has made poetic reference to his mother's encouragement of making up stories. Folk lore in America also emphasizes the feminine schoolmarm, Abe
Lincoln learning his letters from his mother, and the
general role of the woman as the culture-bearer to
frontier towns, introducing theaters and lectures.
Without minimizing the many individual instances,
such as the training of geniuses (McCurdy, 1960),
where the fathers were important in fostering the
imaginative tendencies of children, the statistically
greater possibility at least for earlier generations has
been that a positive early relationship with the mother
is more likely to lead in both men and women to a
greater disposition towards fantasy skill. A poignant
account of a mother's fostering of such a fantasy development in her child appeared in "Stories," a *New
Yorker* short story by Robert Hemenway. Quite recently the poet W. H. Auden has also in a *New
Yorker* magazine memoir reported his mother's role in
molding his imaginative inclinations. The data of the
Singer and McCraven (1961) and Singer and Schonbar
(1961) studies seem to support this finding to some
extent. Where the mother goes further and establishes
some kind of confidante relationship with her children, such internalized activity may be fostered even
more. Sharaf (1959) found that male college students
who had developed much closer relationships with
their mothers were inclined to be higher in intracep-

tion, using Murray's term, a tendency towards awareness and analysis of inner experience. Clinically, observation indicates that excessive fostering of such an
intimate relationship may lead to Oedipal difficulties
and to serious neurotic problems, along with encouraging imaginative development.

GENERAL PARENTAL INFLUENCES

Establishment of a confidante relationship may be
only one of many ways in which close parental contact fosters imaginative development. The general
atmosphere of the home, the emphasis on reading and
literacy, the degree to which the parents are tolerant
of children's fantasy games and encourage exploratory
play—all of these undoubtedly must play a role in the
enhancement of daydreaming as a skill. Parents who
talk freely of stories or plays, who occasionally engage
in bits of play acting themselves, or who, on occasion,
even if briefly, are willing to engage in make-believe
games with children, may provide the stimulation and
stimulus content for the fantasy play the children will
engage in later when alone.

The importance of the stimulus content provided
by parents should not be overlooked. Parents whose
conversation either with each other in the child's presence or directly with the child is limited only to the
most immediately experienced content—"the lateness
of supper," "time for bed," "the window shade needs
fixing," "keep quiet so we can hear the TV!"—are
offering little material which the child can weave into
fantasy play later. Parents who read and tell each
other or the children about the material read or who
discuss significant events not immediately available to
the child—international affairs, their business or work

situations, or even gossip—are providing a greater variety of material. Even when much of this is not well understood by the children, it can be woven into their solitary play; indeed, the very strangeness of some of the material or the names or events may challenge the child's interest and lead to what looks to adults like a somewhat bizarre or comical fantasy creation.

Enforced precocity may also lead to a greater degree of fantasy activity. Parents who discuss more adult subjects with their children or who bring the children along on trips, to theaters, or social engagements intended for adults, are providing some degree of more complex material which children, in imitation initially, and later during assimilative activity, will include in play. Of course, such enforced precocity may not be an optimally healthy situation for a child psychologically. Parents who enforce early social maturity often do so out of coldness, egocentricity, or impatience with childhood's limitations. At the same time, considerable anecdotal evidence indicates that children subjected to such situations often show greater fantasy development. On the other hand, enforced precocity *without* the opportunity for solitary play and practice of fantasy will not lead to an inner development. Children led into professional careers as actors or entertainers have considerable pressure on them for "grown-up" behavior and contact with adults. In their free time, however, they are likely to be required to engage in pre-established training routines, with only very little opportunity for solitary play and imaginative development.

Daydreaming skill is probably closely associated with exploratory tendencies. Parental attitudes that inhibit such activities are also more likely to limit the use of new-found content for fantasy play or the use of fantasy play itself as a technique for creating new environments. Exploration and as-if play both depend on the individualized activity of the child. If excessive parental anxiety, punitive restriction, or contempt block a child's exploration, whether of his body, his environment, or his assimilative play activity, then there is a greater likelihood that he will avoid or be unable to enjoy or attend to private experiences.

For persons whose exploration has been restricted or who are from early years intimidated about assimilative activity, one might expect less discriminating sensitivity even to sensuous experience, as Schachtel (1959) has suggested. Kaplan and Singer (1963) have carried this conception further and argued that what they term a "self-alienated man" would "de-emphasize . . . autocentric modalities and in doing so reduce subjective experience and awareness of self." They hypothesized that a person who rated high on the Rokeach Dogmatism Scale, indicating that "the individual . . . is closed to or unaware of his feelings, tendencies, impulses, or reactions" (Kaplan and Singer, 1963, p. 487), would also reveal less sensory acuity than a person in a contrasted low-dogmatism group. The investigators' results clearly supported their hypothesis that the less dogmatic at the ideational level were also more discriminating at all sensory levels, but particularly in the senses least capable of objective expression, that is, smell, taste, and touch.

This investigation appears to support the view presented here that development of sensitivity to inner experience may be linked with an early opportunity for free exploration, and play may be linked with the opportunity for the utilization of a variety of sensory modalities. A widespread popular point of view, often cited by clinicians as well, holds that the daydreamer or inner-oriented person is less capable of enjoying sensual or physical experience. This notion may have arisen because such persons, who allot greater priority of responding to internal channels, may not overtly manifest their sensual interests to the same degree as persons minimally concerned with inner experience. That such introversive persons are acutely aware of many kinds of sensual experience seems undeniable, however, and in the realm of the creative the great introspectionists have excelled because they were capable of describing with clarity a great variety of subtle taste, smell, and touch experiences, as well as auditory and visual ones. Recall the imagery of Keats's *Eve of St. Agnes*, Joyce's detailed communication of smell and bodily sensation, and, perhaps most strikingly, that the creator of Hamlet also created Falstaff.

The parent, then, in permitting free play and free exploration, establishes a basic atmosphere in which the child can maximize his affective experiences of interest and joy through a series of detailed discriminations. If such discriminations are also incorporated in fantasy play, they become more and more the stuff of a richly sensitive inner experience. Certain areas of experience may be more or less emphasized, of course, by idiosyncratic factors. For example, parents who prevent sexual exploration may be more tolerant of other types of physical exploration. In many subtle ways the parents do indeed play a role in shaping the degree to which exploratory behavior and as-if play will be combined eventually into the cognitive skills of daydreaming and self-awareness.

Opportunity for Practice and Daydream Development

The development of a skill as subtle as the ability to respond to inner spontaneous cognitive processes without necessarily seriously impairing adaptive environmental awareness undoubtedly takes considerable practice. Because of its nature, such a skill must as a rule be practiced alone. The literature on the imaginative, sensitive child has indeed stressed his loneliness, and Schachter's (1961) work on affiliation motivation seems to bring out clearly that first-born or only children do indeed show a craving for company in their fantasy and in some of their actions. Yet children will often show signs of a need to withdraw from a group in order to carry on fantasy activity or some form of solitary play or, later on, to read or to engage in a hobby. Our present American society in many ways offers little such opportunity, however; the great emphasis on organized activity—the round of Brownies or Cub Scouts, music lessons, dance lessons, Little League games, father-son dinners—precludes the privacy a child needs for solitary play and fantasy development.

Quite apart from any active part played by parents, other factors may significantly affect the opportunity for practice of fantasy. An only or first-born child may, of course, have the greatest opportunities for solitary play since even doting parents must spend some time on adult preoccupations. But the second-, third-, or fourth-born child (except in cases of a great age gap with other siblings) is in quite a different psychological situation. Other children represent a constant element in his life space, and the likelihood of his being left alone is greatly reduced. The active play of other children has a strong appeal and leads a child to give up solitary play rather readily. The level of imagination in play groups tends as a rule towards that of the least imaginative unless there are older children in leadership or unless the more imaginative children are also particularly forceful personalities. Observing attempts at organizing more elaborate fantasy play games among groups of five- through eleven-year-old children can be painful for adults who see the efforts of the children trying to plan the game interrupted by sudden laughter or irrelevant teasing and chasing. The experience of such group situations has unquestioned value for a child in preparing him for the comparable ebb and flow that occurs in adult conversations and social behavior, but it may be destructive of the development of imaginative skills.

Indeed, such a realization undoubtedly affected the thinking of parents intent on producing genius children, for a number of them insisted on the child's complete separation from peer groups (McCurdy, 1960). John Stuart Mill has written with sadness of the social harm done him by his father's early intellectual program for him, but it is quite clear that the program did have its effect of producing an active intraceptive capacity. Bertrand Russell has also described a long period of social isolation in childhood when he lived with his grandmother and found most of his stimulation in self-created games and his library (Egner and Dennon, 1962).

The opportunity for privacy thus permits time for practice of self-generated play or later daydreaming skill. Such private activity also must play a great part in leading to a highly differentiated sense of self or of "me-ness." The very act of observing one's own inner processes or of creating play situations in which no others are sharing makes for a more sharp differentiation of the I-thou dimension, and, incidentally, of the dimension of inner experience as a clearly delineated sphere of activity. In moderation such separation of self may be an essential feature of a healthy development of self-awareness and individuality. Of course, it can be carried too far—to the point of a schizoid solipsism. At the other extreme, the child who is never alone may later in life find it difficult to be in situations in which he is socially isolated and may be startled when he is made aware of his ongoing inner spontaneous processes. The finding cited by Mendelson (West, 1962) that hallucinators showed less daydreaming predisposition than did nonhallucinators, suggests that one adaptive advantage of the practice of daydreaming is that it prepares the adult to accept his own inner processes and to differentiate fantasy from reality more precisely.

The accident of birth into the middle of a large family, the fate of growing up in conditions of lower socioeconomic status or severe poverty, where crowded conditions prevail, may impede development of sensitivity to inner experience. The so-called inability to delay gratification, impulsivity, and lack of basic trust manifested by many children from culturally disadvantaged groups may in part reflect the lack of inner continuity and integrated self-differentiation which an opportunity for the development of an inner fantasy life might have been able to provide. Growing up in an atmosphere where parents themselves present

models of aggressive, uneducated, impulsive, or dis-
trustful behavior (Mischel, 1965), children may be less
likely to internalize long-range goals or fantasy play
content. In this connection the influence of television
as a stimulant of fantasy may be quite significant, but,
unless the material provided is assimilated when the
child is alone, the TV content may ultimately be
available only when he directly confronts the set itself.

Cultural Stimulation of Imagination

Reading, radio serials, television, movies, and popular
music undoubtedly all play an important role in stimulating fantasy play in young children and daydreaming
in later childhood and adolescence. These media undoubtedly encourage the actual engagement in as-if
behavior. Thus the very young child, even in watching a TV cowboy movie, may arise and begin to play
his own cowboy game with shouts and "giddyaps" and
"bang-bangs," soon losing contact with what is actually transpiring on the screen. The popular entertainment media make available scenes of interpersonal
behavior, places, and events ordinarily beyond the
intellectual grasp of younger children but exciting
enough to suggest imitation or assimilative play. For
the child from a family which presents a drab or even
noxious model, such popular fantasy stimuli present
dramatic alternatives. The models presented by television and movie stars or popular singers undoubtedly
influence styles of dress, speech patterns, and to some
extent, personality characteristics. The exotic or lux-

urious settings of movies and television and the interesting characters portrayed provide basic content for
fantasy activity.

An interesting question is whether reading is more
stimulating to the development of imaginative skill and
reliance on inner experience than, say, radio, movies,
and television, in approximately that order. In general,
adolescents who show active and varied fantasy lives
tend to be more extensive readers but we cannot be
sure whether a causal aspect is involved. One might
speculate that a medium such as reading, which permits greater reliance on the various imagery modalities, leads to more development and skill at reliance on
inner channels. I believe radio played an immediate
role in this regard, since visual imagery had to be developed somewhat to follow the direct auditory stimulation of the story. The tremendous power of the
movies and of television in exciting fantasy activity
cannot be denied, however. The ready availability of
television and movies leads also to the young person's
reliance on them *instead* of carrying on individual fantasy activity. In that case, the extensive practice and
time required to miniaturize perceptual and motor
imagery into forms suitable for extended storage does
not take place and the capacity for a self-generated
daydream does not develop to the same extent as it
does for a reader who takes time to think about the
material in a page and run it through a "mental
screen."

Popular songs may be mentioned briefly. Much has
been written about their content as a reflection of
adolescent fantasies and as a stimulant for such fantasies. While my introspections as a music lover make
it clear that much daydreaming occurs during music

listening, it is also the case that when an extended daydream is touched off a good deal of the music is missed! The popular song to which most adolescents listen word for word with concurrent dancing or foot-tapping or active singing calls forth a direct perceptual-motor reaction. Such direct motor responses do not seem especially conducive to developing inner fantasy skills. The definite psychological values of music lie, I believe, not so much in the encouragement of inner-directed orientation as in the very direct physical, perceptual, aesthetic response.

Although we have little formal evidence, it seems quite likely that subcultural group experience plays a significant role in imaginative development. If the cultural atmosphere reflects hostility towards imaginative play, it may affect the way in which a child sees such activity as ego-syntonic. Studies by Singer and Opler (1956) and Opler and Singer (1956) yielded some indications that anthropological suggestions concerning the support of fantasy in Irish and Italian cultures were upheld in a group of schizophrenics. McArthur's (1955) study of the fantasies of upper-class and middle-class adolsecents also revealed differences in value orientation and in relative emphasis on past versus future, but little evidence on the effect of class status on degree of fantasy is available.

A fairly general trend in the American ethos has been a distrust of the fantastic and highly imaginative, perhaps as one aspect of a strong anti-intellectual facet of our society. Such a trend has never been completely dominant, however, despite viewers-with-alarm in every generation. After all, America has produced such highly imaginative writers as Poe, Hawthorne, Melville, and Faulkner. It remains to be seen whether the great upsurge of respect for the scientist as a man of great inner capacity will affect the anti-imaginative facets of our society. Since the orbiting of Sputnik, the PTA's and school boards and congressmen have become more interested in "creativity," most especially of the type exemplified by the thinking-man, engineer, or scientist daydream pattern described in the Singer and Antrobus (1963) factor analysis (see pp. 75-78).

Since teachers, counselors, fellow-students, and others still reflect the dominant distrust of daydreaming in our society, one might expect the adolescent to be less developed in this skill and to quell any tendency in himself toward fantasy. Complex forces are at work in our society, however, and the great recent interest of the brighter high-school students in the "beat," in existential concepts or "Zen," undoubtedly reflects an effort to assert their right to develop their own imaginations without the contempt from others usually forthcoming to the dreamer. The very fact that in psychology there has been enough recent interest in such inner processes so that experimental papers on dreaming or fantasy processes (outside of strictly clinical concerns) are beginning to appear, undoubtedly reflects some small inward turn of the mores!

Suggestions for Further Research

It should be obvious to a critical reader that what has been asserted in this chapter remains far too general and that much greater precision in theoretical formulation and experimental study is necessary. The use of inner and outer channels (following the computer model of Chapter 5) meshes with concepts such as Piaget's *assimilation* and *accommodation*, or Schachtel's *autocentric* and *allocentric* perceptual modes. All of these formulations involve dichotomies that may be too gross to describe the cognitive dimension in question. By defining fantasy play carefully, for example, in terms of relative nonperceptual elements, we could observe children under specified conditions of drive or affective arousal and ascertain whether fantasy play does indeed occur most often under minimal biological drive pressure. The degree of fantasy introduced into children's play during a period of hunger (prior to lunch, for example) compared with such elements manifested following a meal, might be observed systematically with suitable controls. Or one might study the manner in which systematically presented novel elements in an otherwise very familiar environment are integrated into fantasy play. A more systematic study of birth position and the degree of as-if elements in play would be most desirable, too.

Female readers may be aware that most examples in this book describe boys' experiences. Girls usually play games such as "house" and "school" that prepare them for normal adult roles, while the boys' games more often involve unreal possibilities. Both types of play call for as-if elements but have different implications for socialization. Adult data suggest no sex differences in frequency or even in content except for the most obvious ones of heroism for males versus fashion interest for females. Much needs to be done in this field with children, however.

A whole area as yet unexplored is that of trying to train children to play fantasy games and observe the degree to which internalization does occur. Ideally it would be desirable to see whether a long-term plan of such training would lead to greater internalization and sensitivity to inner channels in adolescence. One might also set up a graded series of such training for children and early adolescents and observe closely how the different age groups go about learning to fantasize. One might predict greater motor and perceptual behavior in the younger groups and increased evidence of compression and miniaturization in the fantasy-play learning of the adolescents. By careful observation of actual play and then comparison with the children's behavior in suitably modified monitoring or vigilance situations, we might begin to catch hold of the degree to which an ongoing inner stream of imagery is already present well before adolescence. It would also be possible to compare the degree of motor elements in spontaneous play with the degree of imagery manifested under reduced sensory stimulation.

Chapter

7

TOWARD A THEORY OF DAYDREAMING: ADOLESCENT AND ADULT YEARS

Adolescent Fantasy

In Western civilization daydreaming is regarded as a special characteristic of adolescence. Serious and popular literature are full of references to the adolescent lost in fantasies, weaving varied multicolored pictures of heroic achievement, travel to distant lands, or romantic fulfillment. The adolescent is often depicted in cartoons, movies, or illustrations for popular magazine stories as curled up in a chair staring off into space, engaged in active contemplation of complex imagery relating to his or her future, or reminiscing in the winter about a summer flirtation.

One of the few systematic studies of adolescent fantasy, that by Symonds (1949), with its follow-up by Symonds and Jensen (1961), relied heavily on a thematic apperception technique. It is certainly clear that the major themes one might expect emerge in these stories—concern with achievement, future roles, and sexual attainment. The data, however, tell little of the *structural* characteristics of daydreaming in adolescents. Is it indeed more frequent than in adults? Is it purely wish-fulfilling? Does it prepare for future roles? To what extent is it a pathological manifestation and what forms of adolescent fantasy are indeed malignant? We really have few clear answers to any of these questions. Perhaps the most significant result of the Symonds and Jensen (1961) follow-up study is the finding that many adolescent fantasies do come true; the dominant themes of adolescent stories emerge in aspects of the actual vocational choices of the adult some years later.

Let us begin here by considering in more detail some of these structural questions about daydream frequency and pattern. The questionnaire data obtained by Singer and McCraven (1961) indicated the highest self-reported frequency of daydreaming in the adolescent group. The interviews with college students carried out for the Singer and Antrobus (1963) factor analysis also brought out a consistent report from the entering freshmen. They commented that daydreaming in their own lives had reached a peak of frequency within the past two or three years (fourteen to seventeen) but had shown a rather sharp decline during the first months of college. Later interviews with some of the same students and others also confirmed, at least for this group of highly intelligent, well-educated young men, a comparable peaking of fantasy in mid-adolescence and a decline under the great pressure of college work.

In the previous chapter it was stressed that at about

age twelve or thirteen considerable internalization of fantasy play occurs. The use of drawings or the socialized aspects of fantasy play (for example, group games of pirates or cops and robbers or World War battles) are inhibited as a result of social pressure and of the greater crystallization of play along adult-organized lines, such as sports, scouts, music, and dancing. At age twelve or thirteen the greatest degree of miniaturization and compression occurs—and with this, if it is successful, the adolescent discovers a striking new realm of experience over which he or she is likely to seek mastery. This capacity to produce images, to rework the unpleasant, or to contemplate the future in the complete privacy of one's mind may be a discovery for many of greatest importance. Its occurrence is too gradual for it to be noted as a specific event, although individuals interviewed did report some distinct sense of excitement at the dawning realization that they could create a private world without social embarrassment.

As a consequence of the increased differentiation of interests and skills that characterizes growth, one might also anticipate that the degree and type of internalization might reflect more specific cognitive styles. Thus one might expect to detect even in the fantasy play of the child more specific patterns emerging. For example, some girls will be found to focus on travel adventures for their dolls, others to emphasize fashion; some boys will put greater emphasis on sports fantasies, and others on science fiction or "monsters." There is, however, despite some indications of early style differences, considerable overlap and lack of differentiation, the more imaginative children showing a greater range of content rather than merely a greater percentage of time spent on a delimited fantasy area.

The adolescent may show more clearly a differentiation of pattern along the lines of the objective-
controlled thought versus fanciful, interpersonally-
oriented daydreaming dimension which emerged in
the Singer and Antrobus (1963) factor analysis. The
objectively oriented or scientifically or mechanically
gifted adolescent may find himself imagining construction of equipment, or thinking about how one
"soups up" a hot rod. He is also likely to see himself
showing off the hot rod to his friends or to a special
girl or imagining himself winning a prize for some
scientific invention. More personal elements continue
to enter into the daydreams of the objectively oriented, impersonally curious adolescent. Even natural scientists report that personal imagery intrudes
on their normally objective thought. Role differentiations and particular skills and talents thus influence
content, although obviously underlying motive patterns, such as achievement and sex, characteristic of
the adolescent period, also reflect themselves here.

The budding popular singer imagines her success in
a smash musical show and winning a handsome husband; the young athlete, a professional career and the
pretty cheerleader as his "steady"; and the young
scholar envisions a Nobel Prize and a brilliant, lively,
Swedish bride (if he has been seeing Bergman movies!). The less clearly wish-fulfilling daydream does
occur with some frequency in adolescence, too—the
tortured self-concern and ethical questioning found in
the Singer and Antrobus (1963) study, as well as the
body-oriented, anxious fantasy. These negative types
of daydreams seem to get more time allotted to them
by those in older age groups, a clear reflection of the

vicissitudes and disappointments imposed by the reality of adult experience. But they are already present in adolescence and reflect the questioning and doubts, the *Sturm und Drang* of this period.

The increase of daydreaming generally in adolescence (not yet confirmed across subcultural groups, however) undoubtedly reflects a continuation of the children's world of play, now internalized completely, and the awareness of and promise of the adult future which cannot yet be translated into action. Stimulation in movies, songs, books, and more complex educational material arouses new, adult interests and coincides with growing internal sexual development. The imitative accommodation of the child which provided content used in assimilative play is mirrored next in the adolescent's attempted imitation of the adult sexual role or material and intellectual achievements. The adolescent's assimilative efforts provide content for his new-found capacity for imagery and fantasy.

Some adolescents transform quasi-imitation of the adult stimulus pattern into a fantasy expression, while others, lacking fantasy skills or defenses, manifest overt imitation. The precocious early dater who is "going steady" by the eighth grade may not actually be more sexually developed or interested in the opposite sex than the bookish thirteen-year-old who has no overt social expression. Often enough the early dating pattern reflects two factors. In the first place, sexual inclinations as part of normal maturation are likely to exert more pressure on the child who has an initially limited repertory of interests and cognitive capacities. The great adult-world focus on sexual behavior, fostered through advertising, parents' overidentification with children, and popular music, is more likely to seem a chief source of interest and pleasure. On the other hand, the adolescent with a greater cognitive exploratory tendency may have already carved out a greater diversity of behavioral activities—athletics, intellectual achievements, musical skills, or other hobbies—which provide attraction and joy. For these children increased internal glandular and social pressures for sexual behavior seem less prominent in the motive hierarchy.

The second factor represents a difference in internalization capacity. The adolescent who cannot provide himself pleasure through internal fantasy, contemplation, or manipulation of daydream images is compelled more directly to an overt motor imitation of the adult pattern. He undoubtedly has sexual fantasies at times, but he may be ashamed of these on grounds of various cultural or early family experiences; or—and this point has largely been neglected —lacking the experience in fantasy play, he may be unable to elaborate on his fleeting images to make them really interesting. Even masturbation, which produces specific pleasure, may appear less satisfying for the adolescent who lacks capacity to elaborate in the imaginative realm on romantic situations and sexual partners. The pressure towards direct sexual experience is greater for the extroverted adolescent. Such activity, while unquestionably of great value in providing social skills and cognitive abilities in *direct* interpersonal situations, also produces behavior more likely to distract from schoolwork, threaten the adult world, and hasten pressures such as early marriage, for which he is not yet prepared.

The example chosen has stressed sexual activity, but it might apply quite as well to other forms of pressure on the adolescent for adult imitation. For example, competence strivings make the pressure to drive a car quite great, and in individual cases this may be enhanced by symbolic sexual or power associations. Here again, the adolescent with a greater breadth of interests and a capacity for fantasied self-stimulation may experience a comparable excitement and urge to drive but it becomes only one of a variety of interests or can be internalized into a more complex daydream pattern. The youth lacking such alternatives moves more directly to the involvement with cars, often with positive benefits in the development of mechanical skills and motor capacities. He may also risk the ire of adults and endanger his own life because his awareness of the dangers of driving does not match his already mature motility skills.

Spivack and his collaborators (1964) recently studied middle-class adolescents who had a history of conflict with parents, school, and legal authorities. These young people were compared with otherwise similar adolescents of equivalent I.Q. and socioeconomic status, but with no history of delinquency. In a test of story completion, the delinquent group showed less awareness or ability to describe the intermediate steps or alternatives involved in a goal-directed behavioral sequence. They also expressed less awareness of consequences of transgression. The nondelinquent adolescents manifested an equal *interest* in transgression but were more capable of describing pros and cons and even of looking for loopholes. On another measure based on the Rorschach, the more delinquent group showed consistent poverty of idea elaboration. As Spivack put it: "Their thought world appears as a rather barren place" (pp. 5-6). Of particular interest in the light of the discussion of parental stimulation of fantasy play in the previous chapter is the finding that these delinquent adolescents showed a constriction in both future and past temporal perspective. They knew little of their family history and background, or fathers' work, and they made unrealistically hasty estimates of how long it would take for certain events to occur in the future. The impression given by Spivack's report is that there had been surprisingly little interaction with parents or discussion of adult concerns, past or future, which might have stimulated a more differentiated imaginative response as one aspect of the child's accommodation-assimilation pattern.

For some adolescents, then, the degree of cognitive skill is an additional element in explaining the increased daydream activity of that general period. As with the child, free time is also an important element. Despite school and social activities, the general freedom from extensive responsible work of the adult's world for most adolescents simply leaves blank spaces in their days when fantasy activity can be practiced.

Closely related to the factor of time in the sustenance of fantasy is the element of direct reality-experience. There is a subtle and complex relationship which some day may be stated mathematically between the direct perceptual experience of an event and one's capacity to sustain a daydream about it. Children engage in fantasy games based on TV and movies in which they casually mow down enemies with machine guns or drop bombs on cities. To the adult who has experienced combat and war, such thoughts, brought on by watching children play, are often almost painful because he has stored in his memory scenes of actual death and destruction. "He jests at scars, that never felt a wound," as Romeo says. Some disturbed adults may continue to relive war experience in fantasy but with pain and distress and rarely in the joyous fashion which children manifest. Yet long before children have experienced any of war's destruction, they begin to relinquish fantasies of such military activity. Other manifestations of reality thus enter to prevent the maintenance of a fantasy so remote from experience.

For the adult who once wanted to be a great violinist but has had to settle for being a vacuum-cleaner salesman, the recurrence of the "violin" fantasy brings pain at the realization of its improbability, where once it might have brought joy and excitement. For the adult, many of life's possibilities are now sharply delimited and the continuation of fantasies about impossible alternatives can be distressing. Daydreams gradually move more and more along channels of well-established commitments—marriage, work, family possibilities—with only an occasional fling into the improbable, generally fostered by television or movie presentations.

There may well be a significant number of persons —for example, those who score high on the general daydreaming factor in the Singer and Antrobus (1963) study—for whom daydreaming itself is a sufficiently pleasurable realm so that they can tolerate a great variety of improbable thoughts. Daydreaming thus functions as a general reinforcer. It seems likely, however, that a crystallized or recurrent fantasy which lacks some degree of external stimulus nutriment will not be sustained. A person with a style calling for high priority of attention to inner cognitive channels might think fleetingly of what it must be like

to be the Duke of Edinburgh and cast himself temporarily in that role, but it is unlikely that he would
continue such a fantasy very long or that it would
recur in the way some of the personal early adolescent
fantasies I have described appear to do.

The pain of adolescence may stem in part from the
frequency with which fantasies of that period are
tested against reality and must be given up within a
short span of years. A girl may have fantasies which
include an image of herself as particularly beautiful, as
a fashion model, a successful popular singer, the most
popular girl in the school, the steady of a very desirable fellow she knows, the unassailable virgin until marriage, the wife of a brilliant scientist, the wife of a
dashing movie star, the devoted mother of a fine family, and the dynamic career woman. Between the ages
of seventeen and twenty many of these dream balloons
may be punctured, and in fact the whole delicately
balanced structure may collapse as commitments take
place and a very different life appears in the offing.
The adolescent who has a variety of fantasies but who
can also sustain at least some of them by promising
achievement or actual successful experience is able to
give up many of his fantasies with less distress and to
retain enough of them so that fantasy itself is not a
frightening dimension of behavior which must be
avoided. In clinical work with adolescents I have observed that if one can gain the confidence of a young
person and elicit fantasies and then explore with him
his areas of competence or potential reward which
bear on some of these fantasies, this bitter and painful
relinquishment of fantasy (often associated with depression or impulsive "acting-out") can be somewhat
minimized.

The young person who has, through parental contact or other adult models, through travel or good reading and education, managed to differentiate the realities of future possibility may modify fantasy accordingly and may be able to elaborate the means-end cognizances so essential for effective planning. One of the most painful experiences of the Harlem adolescent* is the fact that television and movies and the somewhat improved economic possibilities for Negroes sustain an increased variety of fantasies into adolescence, but in the reality of Harlem ghetto and slum, such high hopes soon turn to ashes in the mouth; bitterness and resistance to further introspection may follow. Where, however, the real possibility exists as evidenced from parents' or teachers' attainment and from reading or travel, the incorporation of reality into the adolescent daydream actually sustains fantasy and, by feedback, aspiration, and also makes possible the use of inner experience to buffer the stress of adolescence.

In summary, then, relatively high frequency of adolescent fantasy may be sustained by a series of conditions:

1. The continuation into adolescence of the child's self-generated fantasy play tendencies;

2. The experience of multiple adult role possibilities which stimulate accommodation through imitation and which are assimilated into the new-found capacity for *internalized* fantasy play;

3. The already established degree of differentiation in interests and in exploratory behavior;

4. The actual skill already established in shifting rapidly between direct perception and response to

* Dr. Kenneth Clark, personal communication.

inner channels or symbol and image manipulation, the daydreaming capacity;

5. The degree of differentiated external stimulus content obtained through varied parental or sibling interests and communication, travel, reading, interesting adult contacts;

6. The sheer amount of time available for engaging in free fantasy, unlimited by pre-established channels of thought such as are forced on adults by economic or family responsibility;

7. The degree to which lack of contact with reality at first makes possible complex associative combinations and fantasy aspirations and later the degree to which reality contact or actual performance is sufficiently related to the daydream to sustain its recurrence without arousing pain or anxiety.

The daydreams of the adolescent are a basic part of his growth process. If the adolescent can effect some combination of actual achievement with the continuation of a varied and increasingly elaborate, but partially reality-oriented daydream life, he can move into adult life armed with a significant skill with important adaptive potential.

Daydreaming Through the Adult Years

With the responsibilities and commitments of maturity, man faces a marked delimitation of the various possibilities in life, and, within this narrower sphere of activity, a greater necessity for attention to detail. The young girl could entertain thoughts of marriage, career, and travel simultaneously because for her, marriage, like most movie endings, involved a kiss, a bridal gown, and "happily ever after." One need not detail the error of such a vision; in effect, once married, the young woman of modest means finds herself plunged into a host of day-to-day activities most of which she may have known about from observing her mother, but which, lacking a comparable commitment, she was ordinarily able to avoid thinking about in detail.

The hours of the day thus require of the responsible man or woman direct perceptual attention to detail or to very specific, task-relevant thought. But even the task-irrelevant daydream is somewhat narrowed in scope. A woman, while diapering her baby, may find herself drifting off into thoughts about what to cook for supper, how to convince her husband that they need a washing machine, or what fun it would be to go to the Couples' Club dance if only she can get reliable Mrs. Eccleston to baby-sit. She is far less likely to drift off even fleetingly into fantasies of dancing the *merengue* with a handsome tanned stranger in the moonlit and palm-swaying setting of a West Indies resort.

Her husband, too, depending on his job, will be markedly more limited in the scope of his daydreams. He may not be immune to fleeting thoughts of sexual adventures with passing beauties on the street or with girls at work, but most of his extended inner activity will be crystallized around job demands, meeting economic pressures, or keeping up with chores around the apartment or home. He may within this narrower range have daydreams of promotion, of telling off his supervisor, or of the dire consequences of a failure in performing some task properly. He is less prone to drift into an elaborate daydream of becoming a military hero, or the first man to reach another planet, or the great young wizard of Wall Street and habitué of Café Society, if he has now become fairly deeply involved in the wholesale furniture business with his father-in-law.

Within the more cystallized cognitive realm of maturity, the predominant daydreaming modes (except in cases of pathology or severe dissatisfaction with job and marriage) have functional significance. For the young woman the thought of what to cook for dinner or the evening ahead with her husband may vary the monotony of the routine of baby care. Her annoyance at the baby for soiling so soon after a fresh change, her never-overcome repugnance for the smell and sight of feces, have created a persisting high density of neural firing and consequently a foul mood or affect of distress or anger. The intrusion of the fantasy about supper, with its arousal of interest-affect, or her daydream about the dance, or the stimulation of contact with her husband, may alter her mood and by providing some brief moments of more positive affect, permit her to return her attention to the baby with less annoyance and more ability to smile and play with the child. The capacity for fantasy thus serves to break up a high level of negative affect, permits a more flexible response to an immediate task, and also prepares for a more planful and flexible future course of action, even within the mundane world of the hard-pressed young homemaker. The woman lacking such daydreaming skill must put up with the ongoing negative affect and may reflect her anger by rough handling of the child or bitter words or by failure to smile and play with the baby. She may seek to break her mood later by motor habits such as smoking, nibbling sweets, or (perhaps more adaptively) by plunging into some more creative home activity as quickly as she can, if the time is available.

Before the reader feels this all verges on a TV domestic comedy-situation series, let me insist on the fact that before turning to the more "glamorous" aspects of daydreaming we must recognize the significant role of daydreaming within the actual routine and monotony of most persons' lives. Much of our attitude about daydreams has come from the fascinating case histories of the psychoanalysts, based, often enough, on most unusual people, or from the accounts of talented writers who have imaginative capacities far beyond the average. Molly Bloom's daydreams, so wonderfully presented by Joyce, interest us because the author is able to show how much indeed can go on in the mind of an otherwise not terribly interesting woman. But Joyce didn't bother to write, as a sequel, another day in the inner life of the Bloom family! One was quite enough. Instead, he plunged into the dream life of H. C. Earwicker for his next effort. Yet the role of daydreams in the life of the mature adult remains an intriguing scientific question. The examples I have chosen reflect how in reasonably integrated persons the capacity for fantasy may function adaptively and even, in a limited way, creatively. The young worker may think of better ways of doing his job or of more interesting future recreations which make a routine job more tolerable. The housewife may think of more effective ways to distract restless children on rainy days and minimize her angry screaming at them.

The adult usually cannot afford too deep an immersion in inner channel response except when preparing for sleep or in a job situation that by its nature permits extensive thought. He can, however, pace his thought to well-established overt response sequences, so that no serious danger is involved. This is possible with minimal risk in many driving situations, when traffic is light, the road clear, and speed moderate. Another opportunity to daydream may be the ride up in an elevator, which permits even a wan smile and a "Hot enough for you?" to the operator while a fantasy or planning sequence unfolds internally.

One's role in life, the degree of direct perceptual and motor co-ordination involved at all times in a job, of course make for sharp differences in the degree to which such pacing is possible. A construction worker high up in the steel work of a skyscraper can afford far less attention to inner channels in his daily work than the architects or draftsmen who sit in offices planning the structure. The speed of alternation of sequences of inner or outer responses thus is clearly a function of social role and vocational or other demands. Stylistic patterns come into play as well; for example, persons who prefer considerably varied external stimulation or who have crystallized habits of an oral nature such as smoking, chewing, or drinking may prefer to rely on these in some situations rather than switching to inner activities. Many persons whose work essentially involves response to inner channels find it necessary to employ some habitual motor activity to vary the activity level. Some philosophers and scientists smoke pipes and by the interminable filling and emptying, cleaning, and lighting up moderate the pace of their internal activity.

Persons whose work requires great visual or auditory concentration or continuous motor activity and who have not developed skill at bringing in occasional fantasy activity or indulging in such activity when their work is done may find themselves extremely rest-less. They may be given to sleeplessness because of excessive ruminative activity when at bedtime they finally delimit sensory activity. Such persons often rely heavily on eating, drinking, smoking, sexual stim-ulation, or late-night television watching. It remains to be seen whether careful electrophysiological studies can provide some indication of the role of imaginal activity in providing for optimal tension or neural fir-ing density levels.

The emphasis on daydreaming in its day-to-day aspects, associated with the humdrum of most lives most of the time, should not obscure other less ordi-nary, sometimes disturbing aspects, even in healthy fantasy. So far I have stressed the "happy family" to bring out the significance of the capacity to resort to inner channels in normal adaptive life. The position I have taken is that daydreaming is a neutral skill avail-able for adaptive enrichment of the life of otherwise ordinary persons as well as being a manifestation in many persons of escape, evasion of responsibility, or self-dissatisfaction. Certain childhood distortions have, however, remained encapsulated in the memory stor-age system and have not had an opportunity to be tested by reality. In such cases unusual or bizarre fan-tasies may persist. Temporary normal deprivations may recall earlier conflict periods and occasion seem-ingly long-forgotten daydreams. The husband watch-ing the attention his wife gets in late pregnancy may be surprised and perhaps frightened by the recurrence of a fantasy of transvestitism or parturition. The up-surge of anger at a boss may revive an early murder-ous daydream plot against a father or older brother. Movies, plays, or television shows, particularly those with family themes, some psychological probing, or dream sequences, unquestionably revive early fantasies. The psychoanalytic process itself represents a technique to establish conditions for a more systematic awareness of unrealistic or bizarre sexual, dependency, or aggressive fantasies. Extreme environmental monotony or heightened conscious efforts to attend to inner channels because of instructions by a psychoanalyst, for example, might also bring into focus a not infrequent association to an early fantasy hitherto largely marginal. The practiced daydreamer may expect such odd thoughts and may experience curiosity rather than anxiety about them. But for many persons unused to noticing the ongoing inner associative stream, the awareness of a suicidal or murderous thought sequence may generate considerable anxiety. A new sequence of painful associations, self-doubts, or fears of action may follow.

Many of these associations or fantasies are probably chance combinations of no great personal significance. Often enough, however, the willingness to stick with an unusual thought or fantasy and to puzzle out its implications or origins may lead to quite original or creative thought. Fromm (1951) and others have argued, for example, that creative thought is inherent in dreams and probably fantasies. I am more inclined to believe that complex associational possibilities necessary for creative thought occur in dreams and fantasies almost by chance and that truly creative work comes in the willingness and effort to explicate such material.

Too often our associations provide us with fleeting clues which we ignore to our own detriment. A person may have a fleeting fantasy that a certain course of action may be deeply insulting or cruel to a friend but fails to elaborate on the thought because of other pressures of the moment. Only later, when the die is cast, he may recall the association with regret at his failure to stay with the thought long enough. Quite apart from the more dramatic or artistic aspects of creativity, such willingness to take the time to examine passing associations may make for more effective prerehearsal of social responses and more creative daily living. For persons such as writers, actors, artists, or scientists, who are engaged in specifically creative endeavor, there is obviously great value in having such heightened sensitivity to the ongoing associative stream or in being willing to play out possibilities or replay past thought sequences in fantasy. For persons whose vocations or obligations demand less of the creative in this respect, the capacity for self-examination can add a dimension of style, excitement, and flair to a life whose main links are with more conventional patterns.

A note of caution on the creative possibilities of fantasy must be brought out in conclusion. I have not meant to suggest that mere willingness to attend to the associative stream suffices in producing creative responses. If a person has shown a basic indifference to distinctions in his environment, if he has accepted cliché meanings, or has lacked interest in exploration, the pattern of stored associations will reflect such constriction. While television unquestionably can provoke adult associations, it can do so far less than real experience, and the combinatory patterns resulting from vicarious experience may be rather stereotyped or cliché-ridden. Self-examination and skill in daydreaming are important assets for most humans but they cannot compensate for restricted and drab life experi-

ences nor can they take the place of extensive reading
or commitment to some cause which involves meaningful experiences. Daydreaming and attention to
inner channels is one of many capacities which can be
developed as part of the development of competencies
and the exploratory attitude which make for zestful
living. If the positive, adaptive aspects of daydreaming
have been stressed here, it is because their significance
has not been widely noted.

Daydreaming in the Aged

There are as yet no solid data on the fantasy patterns
of the really elderly normal person, although a few
studies have suggested greater poverty of imagination
in the projective test storytelling of this group. The
great tendency toward reminiscence probably reflects
the combination of the fact that old learning is better
retained than new with the increasing sameness and
lack of distinctiveness in the daily routine of most
aged persons. The future generally lacks interesting
prospects about which to fantasize and indeed offers
the threat of considering death if one thinks about the
next few years and their possibilities.

Yet the greater freedom of the older person from an
obligatory sequence of thought or action also affords
more time for inner responsiveness. Some cultures,
such as the middle- and upper-class Hindu society,
permit the family patriarch to withdraw with much
respect into a life of contemplation and detached
philosphical religious speculation, but this is less likely
in Western civilization. Statesmen and generals can
occupy their later years in a socialized reminiscence,

the writing of memoirs or historical treatises, but most elderly persons lack such outlets and, if dwelling with their families, they may soon find their stories falling on bored ears. Where responsibility for the young remains a part of the older person's life, such reminiscences are more welcome and are useful to the child, but this seems less and less a feature of our present society. The aged person who now has the leisure and inclination for at least a reminiscent form of fantasy may soon find himself bored at his own self-recounting of his past, and the apathy and depression that presages senile withdrawal set in.

To the extent that a person has already developed an extensive capacity for response to internal channels, for fantasy play, for speculation or self-examination, the decreased social demands of aging hold less terror. Such a person may continue some form of intellectual activity or hobby and may also turn more and more toward examining the broader ethical, philosophic, or religious meanings of his experiences. He may keep abreast of current events in a personal field of interest such as a fraternal order, church congregation, political club, or professional society, or he may even seek some form of direct involvement by writing letters to editors, for instance. If some such commitment is possible even with the generally greater social disengagement of the retired person or very elderly, the future can be spelled out in imaginative activity. The aged grandmother may still fantasy about the schooling or wedding plans of various grandchildren provided she is kept informed so that her fantasy is strengthened by reality experience. She may speculate about the long-term changes in her growing family and in so doing may provide herself with a sufficiently novel environment to counteract the all-too-familiar routine of her perhaps presently bedridden condition.

Perhaps one area in psychological work with the aged that might be more thoroughly explored would be the degree of active fantasy in the elderly person and its relation to relative adjustment. I suspect from clinical experience that in cases where self-awareness (of a nonhypochondriacal type) can be fostered, along with the ability to engage in the equivalent of fantasy play, speculation, and commitment to some ideational goal, then apathy and depression can be forestalled. The aged person who never developed a taste for inner living may now, with help, be more ready for this experience than he might have been in his middle years. The training for self-enrichment which so often fails with this type of person (who usually rejects psychotherapy) in younger days may be more possible now that many of the "flight into activity" defenses are no longer available. Such training may involve a search for latent interest patterns or long-dead desires which may not be at this age impossible of attainment. Training of an older person towards attainment of such short-term goals may very well enable him to look ahead again and to experience the anticipatory pleasures and joys ordinarily available to the practiced daydreamer. As the sentimental poem goes:

> *Age is a quality of mind—*
> *If you have left your dreams behind,*
> *If hope is lost*
> *If you no longer look ahead*
> *If your ambition's fires are dead—*
> *Then you are old.*

Chapter

8

DAYDREAMING IN PSYCHOPATHOLOGY AND IN DAILY LIFE

It may be useful to the student to suggest briefly some lines along which the study of fantasy processes may touch on the important practical issues of our lives. Alerted to the fact that data are sparse and many gaps exist, the interested reader may discern the possibility of an application to his own situation or to the future development of serious research or scholarship in this field which will make this speculative effort worthwhile indeed.

Psychopathological Considerations

Previous chapters have emphasized the function of daydreaming as either a natural feature of development or as a potential skill available for practice and adaptive use. Such an emphasis has been intentional in order to counteract the more widely held view of fantasy as a defensive maneuver or symptom of severe maladjustment or schizoid tendencies. It would be unfortunate if readers were left with the notion that daydreaming has no pathological implications. It is important to understand the conditions under which fantasy may prove to be maladaptive or self-defeating and also to ascertain for diagnostic purposes what patterns and what degree of such activity ought to be viewed as pathognomic of potential difficulty.

One of the practical obstacles to early diagnosis of serious pathological developments in children lies in our lack of a sufficient base of information on the early manifestations of daydreaming. Clinicians and teachers have perhaps erred too often in attributing pathology to the "shy, withdrawn" daydreaming child or to the evidences of aggressive content manifested in fantasy play. A distinction may have to be drawn between the inattentive, disorganized, and withdrawn child and the child who has begun to develop an active fantasy capacity. Unpublished data from some of the Antrobus and Singer experimental studies suggest that for adolescents, "mind wandering" and daydreaming are not highly correlated. Indeed, mind wandering may reflect an inability to follow a sequence of thought or to avoid response to a variety of external stimuli. The apparently preoccupied child in the class may not necessarily be involved in rumination or inner play, and may be suffering almost as much from the lack of such a capacity as the hyperactive, overly aggressive child. Clinical experience suggests a distinction between the imaginative, quiet child and the disturbed, inattentive child on the basis of variety and richness of responses to inkblots or projective pictures. We do not have sufficient normative data by projective methods on whether early differences in fantasy capacity lead to schizoid patterns by adolescence.

Wagner and Stegemann (1964) recently surveyed studies which trace pathological outcomes of childhood traits. They called attention to confusion in the notion of early schizoid manifestations. Schizoid was defined as a personality disorder involving shyness, withdrawal, emotional inhibition, and *an active fantasy life*. The results of their reanalysis of the findings led to the conclusion that introverted children were *least* likely to end up as schizophrenic and that adult schizophrenics whose earlier school histories were checked more often showed outgoing or mixed behavior, considerable overt motor hyperactivity, antisocial behavior, and other externally oriented responses. According to Wagner and Stegemann's analysis, there are no grounds whatsoever for linking adult schizophrenia with an early history of "shyness," quiet behavior, and daydreaming.

Men have long regarded the mental patient—and particularly the schizophrenic, with his delusions and hallucinations—as dwelling in a "private world" of fantasies and daydreams. Individual schizophrenics during psychotherapy or intensive interview have reported rather elaborate delusional imaginings or bizarre daydreams. These, however, seem the exceptions in the great bulk of severely disturbed mental patients. Probably the assumption of the withdrawal into a world of fantasy stems from the attempt of the relatively normal person to account for the social withdrawal and occasional talking-to-thin-air of schizophrenics. Recalling his own daydream tendencies, the normal person assumes that the patient is doing the same thing even more extensively.

A word may be said concerning the relations of daydreaming to pathological phenomena such as hallucinations or delusions. Hallucinations are apparent perceptual responses which lack any stimulus basis. Except in toxic conditions such as acute alcoholism or brain damage due to poisonings or tumors, the most frequent hallucinations are *auditory* experiences—in marked contrast to daydreams, which are predominantly *visual*. Delusions are false inferences usually based on reasonably accurate perception. A patient, already in doubt about his masculinity, observes two passersby in conversation and assumes that they are accusing him of homosexuality. Delusional thought is probably closer to daydreaming than it is to hallucination. The latter experience seems more characteristic of persons with little evidence of imagination, while delusions occur more in persons with a greater history of imaginative capacity. Opler and Singer (1956), in a comparison of Irish and Italian schizophrenics, found, for example, that the more imaginative, Irish patients were more prone to religious delusions, while the less imaginative, more overtly emotional, Italian schizophrenics more often experienced hallucinations.

The bulk of projective test data (Rickers-Ovsiankina, 1960) fails to provide evidence of greater imaginative richness in schizophrenics; such patients, while showing distortions of reality and false perceptions, tend on the whole to reveal a poverty of associational material or constructive fantasy. Instead of bizarre, imaginative tales of strange happenings, events, or places, one usually gets from a schizophrenic a fragmentary account of suspicions, misinterpretations of recent occurrences, or repetitive accounts of assumed injustices. From Freud's concept of transference and Sullivan's description of the parataxic distortion of the schizophrenic, we can now understand the communication of many schizophrenics as a failure in differentiation between their reactions to parental figures and new responses necessary for dealing with adults other than parents. The bizarre behavior stems often enough from the patient's making a response based on his continued involvement with his parents or childhood needs. His response, no longer appropriate to the person confronting him, sounds fantastic because it is irrelevant from the normal point of view. This distortion of reality is, however, a rather concrete thought pattern and lacks the flexibility or differentiation of most fantasy behavior. That schizophrenics as a group are socially withdrawn seems without question. A study by Singer and Spohn (1956) revealed only a minimal response of acute and chronic schizophrenics to a televised World Series game in marked contrast with active involvement of normal men of the same generation. Interviews with chronic schizophrenic patients suggested that their lack of interest in the game or in their fellow patients was not the result of an absorption in fantasies. Frequently enough they reported paying what seems to a nonpatient like an endless amount of attention to the concrete details of a room, to the burning of their cigarettes, or to the pattern on the dayroom curtains, a kind of glassy-eyed attention to external channels rather than the active creation of an inner fantasy world.

At some point in the course of mental distress, the individual who has already developed a differentiated capacity for inner channel response may become absorbed in fantasy for periods of time. As the emotional disturbance persists, however, hospitalization or other social withdrawal may lead to a "withering away" of the fantasy activity for lack of external stimulation and, perhaps too, because without hope the occurrence of fantasy wishes becomes increasingly painful. Wittkower's (1949) studies of tubercular patients reported an upsurge of sexual daydreams at the onset of hospitalization, with a subsequent disappearance of all fantasy as hope of recovery faded.

Individual cases do exist, of course, where the developing child's excessive resort to fantasy may almost completely substitute for social contact. The result may be failure to develop social skills and sensitivity to the nuances of interpersonal communication. The child who has withdrawn excessively into a fantasy play world which he alone can control may learn too late that he is lacking in such communication and interpersonal skills. He may be overly formal with his peers or perhaps too literary in his conversation. The embarrassment when teased about such formalism may increasingly force him into his inner world. As time passes, social intercourse may appear more and more like an alien activity fraught with the hazards of humiliation. Rationalizing his fear as being a scorn of stupidity or "bourgeois conformity" or on some other, similarly self-deluding basis, he may continue to avoid anything but superficial social contacts.

The danger of serious pathology arising from the excessive and defensive use of fantasy lies not only in the social withdrawal and consequent failure to develop social skills, but also in the extreme elaboration of a conception of social situations which have not been tested in real-life situations. One such example is the fantasy about sexual intercourse which an inexperienced, inhibited, young person may develop out of reading and some little dating. It may be glorified in thought as an experience of such overwhelming excitement and deep romantic communication between the partners that, sensing the unlikelihood of its fulfillment, the daydreamer avoids social activity that may put it to a test. Or, should a situation arise in which intercourse occurs, the lack of the motor component of experience leads to a hesitant performance or a failure which looms all the larger in comparison with the fantasy and hence results in a further withdrawal from attempts in reality.

Because of persisting taboos on sexual activity as well as the general lack of information, certain mistaken attitudes about sex may also be played out again and again in fantasy and may lead to gross misunderstandings or confusion when real sexual activity is imminent or under way. Somewhat related to this is the development of fantasies in masochistic perversions, which have been brilliantly analyzed by Reik (1959). Reik points out the degree to which an elaborated fantasy is an essential component in masochistic sexual behavior and reports his experience that persons who lack imaginative capacities are less likely to be inclined toward masochism. He regards the detailed self-denigrating fantasies of the masochist as a means of punishing oneself in advance for the forbidden sexual activity to occur subsequent to the fantasy. Some women report that before relaxing completely in sexual relations, even with someone they love, they engage in a masochistic fantasy. One relatively "normal" woman informed me that at the onset of sexual rela-

tions with her husband if she engaged in a daydream
of being raped by Communist agents she found her
excitement mounting and her capacity for orgasm increased. An intriguing question in itself is the manner
in which such a vivid fantasy persists even when psychological understanding of its origin is present and
when its psychological necessity seems no longer op-
erative because of improved interpersonal functioning.

Another pattern of daydreaming that has pathological implications is the obsessional ruminative fantasy, a
seemingly involuntary repetition of a scene or image
that cannot be "turned off" at will. Sometimes, as in
the case of a traumatic event, it recurs again and again
with associated painful emotion. A number of persons
reported such experiences at the time of the assassina-
tion of President Kennedy, when they found scenes
from the funeral or the image of the President slump-
ing forward in his seat returning to their thoughts
again and again. More trivial, but equally difficult to
explain psychologically, is the repetitive jingle. Mark
Twain's story of the "Punch brothers, punch with
care, punch in the presence of the passenjare" jingle
that haunted him until he could pass it along is such an
instance.

Sullivan (1953a) has described how obsessional fantasies may be substitutions for frightening thoughts that
one cannot face. The obsessional thought preoccupies
the individual, its triviality frees him temporarily from
contemplating a more threatening memory or anxiety-
producing wish. For example, hypochondriacal rumi-
nations ("I wonder if that stomach twinge is an ulcer
or cancer") may distract many people from recogniz-
ing failures in personal relationships, sexual inade-
quacies, unwillingness to make a deep commitment to

a spouse or to a child. This pattern of fantasy seems most likely to be of the type described by Factor H (neurotic daydreaming) in the Singer-Antrobus (1963) factor analysis. Often the victim of such a persisting obsession is a person whose breadth of daydreaming was already limited. It may be that as psychotherapy increases the capacity to entertain a variety of thoughts, the alternatives to the obsessive thought may increase and gradually replace it. One wonders if systematic practice of other fantasies might also work, but this has not been attempted experimentally.

A daydream of an exciting situation may also have some negative psychological consequences apart from that of distracting the individual from his job. Consider the instance, often rather serious in its consequences, of building up of an elaborate fantasy prior to a much-awaited event. A wife somewhat bored with her housework or harried by bickering children awaits her husband's return from work. She constructs a pleasant fantasy of his romantic entrance, passionate embrace, and words of devotion and reassurance. The husband, on the other hand, having spent his day in a seemingly endless series of frenzied verbal exchanges with customers or supervisors, constructs in his turn a fantasy of the relaxed quiet of his home and of the fine dinner and enveloping feminine warmth that await him. When the husband enters, kicks off his shoes, and slumps wearily in his chair, the disappointed wife may launch (still hoping for rescue) into an angry recital of the day's appliance breakdowns and children's misfortunes. This behavior smashes the man's fantasy of the quiet haven, and a bitter quarrel may ensue. Once such a quarrel begins and snowballs, the parties may hurt each other deeply by recalling old grievances. The origin of the disturbance in unrealized fantasies may go unnoticed.

An important feature of psychotherapy often enough is the clarification to a patient, through careful elucidation of the details of such a quarrel, of the manner in which the recriminations grew out of the failure of two mutually incompatible fantasies to materialize. Indeed, psychotherapy in situations of marital difficulty requires a tracing of the systematic expectations of the partners, the degrees to which vivid fantasies exemplifying these expectations have been elaborated, and the sequence of behaviors of each partner which smashes the other's daydream most painfully.

Psychoanalysis in its intensive scrutiny of internally produced connections and marginal thoughts may really involve an implicit training of the person to increase his capacity for response to internal channels. The "successful" patient is prepared, when he experiences sudden anxieties or engages in symptomatic acts, quickly to reverse his stream of thought over the previous few minutes so that he can detect the particular image, memory, or scene which, perhaps by slightly delayed reaction, triggered a long-standing conflict or fear. In effect, such activity greatly broadens the scope of the person's capacity to deal with his own ongoing behavior and frees him from the apparently automatic behavior that so often characterizes neurosis. The stimulating work of Tauber and Green (1959) has pointed out that the analyst can use his own dreams and daydreams to clarify the marginal attitudes or reactions evoked by the patient. These investigators call attention to ways in which daydream material can be used creatively by both therapist and patient.

Under pressure of need or loneliness some persons hitherto inexperienced in daydreaming become aware of their own stream of thought with a vividness that seems occasionally almost like reality. The experience frightens them and the very distress occasioned by the persisting fear feeds back even more frightening thoughts. If a person unused to fantasy activity becomes aware of occasional thoughts about murdering a loved one, the guilt and fear accompanying such thoughts may be particularly great and he may feel that his thoughts are symptomatic of either serious aggressive trends or of incipient madness. As it turns out, the thoughts may reflect only a temporary annoyance which can be understood after detailed inquiry. Unless, however, the person can be gradually helped to be freer in acceptance of his thoughts as an associative stream whose translation into action he can control, the picture of himself as a hateful person or a potential psychotic may lead to mounting anxiety. In some cases, as in the homosexual panic that often precedes a schizophrenic break, the snowballing fear that a thought must be acted upon leads to a relatively irreversible mounting of distress. In less serious instances, however, where some fantasy resources have already been developed, the individual can indeed be helped to see his thoughts in perspective and to learn to use them as clues or signals rather than reify them as acts or compulsions. Some therapists implicitly assist patients to understand their fantasies in this way, but surprisingly, there is little attention paid to more systematic efforts to deal with fantasy training in psychotherapy.

In discussing some of the psychotherapeutic implications of a developed capacity for daydreaming, it
may be noted that it is possible that persons who already have such a predisposition are more likely to
seek psychotherapy. Once involved in it, they are
more likely to continue. Temerlin (1956) found that
persons who were more flexible and productive in the
first twenty sessions of psychotherapy showed greater
flexibility also in their perception of apparent motion,
while Palmer (1956) found that persons who were
more introversive or imaginative in Rorschach performance were characterized by greater self-awareness. The well-known findings of Schachter (1959)
that first-born or only children are more likely to seek
psychotherapy may reflect not only affiliative needs, as
he suggests, but also the greater imaginativeness of
these individuals.

Mental health workers find their greatest challenge
in what is generally called the "acting-out" or "impulse-ridden" child. This hyperkinetic child with
kaleidoscopic moods, truancy, petty delinquency, or
aggression, defies the best efforts of psychotherapists.
Lacking sufficient capacity to gain pleasure from internally produced cognitive processes, such children
are constantly manipulating the environment, often in
destructive ways, to gain some satisfactions, reduce
their anxieties, or even to satisfy exploratory inclinations.

Underlying these patterns in many cases is a lack of
sufficient internalization of socialized adult values or
of fantasy play and as-if capacities. Lacking parental
models from whom they can learn delaying behavior
as a response to deferred gratification (Mischel, 1965),
or lacking parents who foster imaginative behavior,

they are limited in their behavioral repertoire to external channel priorities. The more benign or trusting approach to parents found generally in imaginative children is lacking.

Recently clinical investigators have begun efforts to determine whether or not imaginative capacities can indeed be "built into" such impulsive children. Such an effort may be ultimately more meaningful than traditional play therapy, which has placed its hopes on resolution of early fears and conflicts. In impulse-ridden children, however, the problem may be one of defective development rather than conflict, and a more systematic quasi-educative procedure may be in order. Such an effort was involved in a few instances of encouraging such children or adolescents to engage in storytelling activities as a presumed substitute for overt action. Probably a number of steps are necessary: enrichment of vocabulary through reward for descriptive behavior and attention to detail, learning to play fantasy games, imitation of teachers or therapists who demonstrate imaginative behavior, and reward for combining imaginative play with delayed gratification. A beginning effort in this connection is being carried out by Dr. Max Talmadge and his staff at the Astor Home for Children, but such techniques will obviously call for special training of teachers and therapists. It remains to be seen whether clinicians can be flexible enough to give up their more traditional emphases and move in the direction of such quasi-educative techniques.

Despite the romantic yearnings of some writers who view our present society as excessively mechanized and automated, the increases in leisure, travel, individual hobby possibilities, and stimulus sources from movies and television have opened the way to a more varied stream of associative activity for the great mass of persons whose attention in past ages was limited to most essential physical satisfactions and great physical drudgery in a setting of monotony. The age that produced the brilliant introspections of a Montaigne was also one in which millions toiled long dull hours in limited environments to permit a lord his leisurely retirement. Education for the new world of greater leisure and varied stimulation which beckons our civilization (if peace can be maintained) must, among other things, make possible the more widespread use of imaginative skill if we wish to avert the creation of a nation of stultified TV viewers.

Early suggestions for incorporation of training in self-sensitivity in education were made by F. M. Alexander (1932) with the endorsement of John Dewey. More recently the late Aldous Huxley (1962b) has argued cogently in articles and in novels such as *Island* that society ought to provide children with opportunities for training in improved *awareness* of both internal and external events. Alert to the dangers of man's knack for avoiding serious contemplation by rapid shifting of attention, Huxley calls for greater skill in direct contemplation. He recommends training in sensitivity to external events, an increased and refined discrimination of the environment of the type discussed by Schachtel (1959) and studied experimentally by Kaplan and Singer (1963). At the same time, Huxley also notes that such an increased sensitivity to external stimulation must be complemented by training in the "wise passiveness" which "followed in due course by wise hard work is the condition of creativity" (Huxley, 1962b, p. 268).

In his novel *Island*, Huxley describes a society which attempts to build such sensitivity into the fabric of its play, work, and education. Even the mynabirds on his imaginary tropical island are trained to say "Attention!" calling on children and adults to engage in more sustained and fuller contemplation of both external and internal stimuli. An interesting feature is his description of training children to create imaginary demons in their mind's eye on whom they can vent anger and frustration as a substitute for overt expression of such affects through aggressive action.

A realistic possibility might be the application to children of some of the ingenious techniques employed by Gordon (1961) in creativity training for industry. His concept of *synectics*, the development of problem-solving groups, employs many well-thought-out approaches for having a group of investigators use their own imaginative, combinatory associational patterns in developing solutions chiefly to industrial problems. A group of persons is presented with a creative task which it sets about solving by four techniques "for making the familiar strange": personal analogy, direct analogy, symbolic analogy, and fantasy analogy. These methods serve to broaden the awareness capacity of the participants and introduce metaphorical, as-if, and playlike features into thought, hopefully maximizing man's use of his unusual associative-combinatory potentiality.

Applied in a careful way to children in an educational setting, it seems likely that some such approach might have value in developing greater freedom in thought—that is, the willingness to accept metaphorical thought or fantasy imagery without, of course, losing contact with the reality-oriented problem. Of course creative teachers may already attempt to foster this approach in children; some will ask first-grade children to think of all kinds of unusual ways to get to school and will encourage them to draw these ways. Gordon's book includes many suggestions on how flexible fantasy thought may enrich thinking about physical objects or the natural world. Encouragement of children's awareness of their dreams and fantasies as a legitimate subject of discussion (albeit not of "wild" pychoanalytic interpretations) may also serve to increase flexibility and openness to inner experience.

Pending research exploration of such techniques adapted to children, the type of radical revision of our curriculum suggested by Huxley seems far in the future. Recent increased attention to the education of the culturally disadvantaged children of the rural areas or urban slums may speed innovation of the curriculum along lines of play and imaginative techniques. The problem of creating an atmosphere in which children who have suffered serious cultural deprivation may enrich their vocabulary and increase their usable flow of abstract concepts or of images from a greater range of sources than their own neighborhood experience calls for considerable ingenuity in engaging their sustained attention and interest. Where teaching machines might prove effective with middle-class, self-regulated youngsters, the use of more open fantasy-play procedures may be necessary for the motorically oriented children of lower socioeconomic background. Bandura's work (Bandura *et al.*, 1961, 1963) on modelling and imitation has suggested that we can look more and more to using the teacher's actions as a basis for teaching as well as her words. The teacher who feels free enough to demonstrate imaginative use of vocabulary or sensitive exploration of her own thought may stimulate a like effort in the children. This can only come about if the teachers themselves possess the freedom and self-awareness to risk using their behavior as a basic element in the educative process. An important role for psychologists in the future may well be to assist teachers' groups in performing just such a function.

The fantasy play of children may also serve as an important guide to their interest patterns. The child who shows a great deal of play involving historical figures may be able to be involved more readily in reading materials or related activities by tying them in with such fantasy interests. Our increasing knowledge of fantasy also suggests the need for some caution in interpreting the content of fantasy. The occurrence of much violence in the fantasy play of a child should not be assumed to imply the danger of overt destructive behavior; on the other hand, neither does aggressive fantasy play preclude such overt violence. More important than content of play seems to be its *structure*. The degree to which the child clearly sees his play *as* play or fantasy, the degree to which a shift back to social responsiveness is possible, the degree of creative elaboration of the story-line as against crude expression of the aggressive content coupled with much overt physical action—all these are important clues as to the likelihood of overt antisocial reactions. Unusually idiosyncratic content of a bizarre nature, obviously related to disturbing family patterns, may provide clues as to specific problems distressing a child, but generally speaking the relationship of fantasy to emotional disturbance is more complex and such interpretations can be misleading.

Fantasy outlets, actual dramatic productions, and storytelling for cathartic purposes have been found to be clinically useful in dealing with children who bring insufficient inner controls to the classroom situation. The socialization of active or aggressive children through athletic activities has long been accepted and has provided our society with its major sports figures; a concomitant program for developing more imaginative capacity by fantasy play or dramatic activities has not been tried to the same degree. Methods such as the fantasy games or the synectics techniques of Gordon (1961) might be employed in formal controlled studies with children chosen as extremes along relevant dimensions, such as inadequate inner controls or easy distractibility. Many possibilities beckon once one regards fantasy or daydreaming as a dimension of experience and frees it from the opprobrium implied in "retreat from reality" or "defense mechanism."

It should be stressed for the final time as this work draws to a close that what clearly is needed is less speculation or assertion but more specific research endeavors. The general tenor of my remaining comments represents a point of view and a philosophical direction, but such comments remain essentially most valuable if they can spur specific investigations to deal with the many issues raised herein. Before indulging in a brief peroration let me therefore urge upon the reader not only caution in accepting what I say, but a skeptical curiosity and inclination to empirical test which are the touchstones and the true excitement of science.

Daydreaming in Daily Life

Let us briefly consider, in conclusion, how the average adolescent or mature adult might put his ongoing stream of consciousness to more effective use. It should be noted first, however, that what is being stressed is not a solipsistic self-absorption that becomes an avoidance of the excitement and challenge of life. Such a direction in the resort to daydreams is in itself pathognomic of difficulty in interpersonal relations, and the recognition of such a trend should alert a person to his need for professional help. Pathology in the United States seems most evident in excessive outer-directedness of attention, failures of sustained attention, the ready acceptance of cliché and stereotype, and the avoidance of refined discrimination in social perception or in thought. The interest among psychotherapists in Zen Buddhism reflects an awareness on the part of the professionals working daily and over long periods with adults of the withering away during the socialization process of sustained attention, pleasure in detail, and scrutiny for its own sake.

As Huxley (1962b) has recognized, the concept of openness to experience, so stressed by Suzuki, Fromm, and Schachtel, among others, must include openness to the ongoing inner stream of thought and imaginative productivity. Tauber and Green (1959) have written a stimulating discussion of the therapeutic use of one's own dreams or marginal thoughts, and excellent discussions of creativity such as that by McKellar (1957) have also demonstrated the many values to be derived from a more flexible and *playful* approach to one's own thought process.

Again a note of caution is necessary concerning the use of one's own associative combinations as creative products. From the attempts of Fromm, Tauber, and others to emphasize the creative elements in dreams as a corrective for the Freudian overemphasis on childish or instinctual components, a cultural impression of the inherent value of such "prelogical" material has begun to develop. The associative stream of a mediocre consciousness may produce somewhat more unusual products than the conscious efforts of the same individual, but they are still not likely to be very interesting to other people.

The material of inner experience can also be useful in enriching interpersonal relationships. Allowing oneself to toy in fantasy with a variety of possible techniques for making conversation with an interesting young lady in an elevator may lead to an intriguing approach rather than a dumb silence or a "Nice weather today." The closeness of fantasy and spontaneous associational combinations to humor must be recognized; the creative use of a humorous association, a pun, or an unusual idea combination may break the monotony of a dull association on a train or a cliché-ridden conversation.

The spirit of play through fantasy may also, if adapted effectively to the rhythm of the demands for external attention, serve as a valuable additional source of pleasure to relieve the monotony of a long or difficult task. If the daydreamer is "on top" of his capacity and can turn it off readily, he can return to a difficult task refreshed. In miniature he has available the change of pace or scenery which is so beneficial a factor in returning to work after a vacation. The fairly brief, paced change of a daydream can have as a secondary

benefit the recall of many tasks, objectives, or obligations which we are likely to forget in the press of
daily affairs. The harried husband may more likely
recall his wife's birthday if he allows himself a pause
for free associative thought during the day. He may
even think of a particularly nice gift, something which
would mean a great deal to her. This idea may have
flitted on the margin of consciousness for some weeks
but given a moment of thought about it he may re-
formulate a plan for procuring the gift, even make the
phone call, or a note on his pad, and then return quite
refreshed and exhilarated to the busy routine of his
work. Had he chosen instead of attending to inner
thought to take his break by listening to a baseball
game, reading the newspaper, or engaging in some
other externally oriented activity, the probabilities
that this small creative interpersonal thought would
emerge might be considerably less.

The art of successful daydreaming lies in the
smooth shifting from external awareness to inner concentration. Such timing makes for an enriched and
varied stimulus pattern that keeps interest affect high
for longer periods and maximizes the affect of joy
through reducing the discomfort of monotony or
anger. To the exploratory approach to day-to-day
activities or scenes one can add an exploration *of* and
through thought and a touch of play to one's work
that make for zestful living.

Inner contemplation is not all bliss by any means,
however. Attention to one's own experience brings
one into contact with the pettiness and evil in oneself,
with the doubts and failures of the past, and the wishful deceptions or vengeances of the future that occur
in fantasies both fleeting and elaborate. The motor-

ically hyperactive person, the kaleidoscopic rapid thinker, or the obsessive, with his involvement in petty detail, can all avoid awareness of the ugliness in themselves or the world or of the ever-present danger of the Bomb. The daydreamer is far more likely to come into contact with associations that arouse realistic fears or moments of deep despair. If he has not retreated from active interchange with others, he can have the best and worst of two worlds. What his increased inner capacity offers him is a fuller sense of being intensely alive from moment to moment, and this may be worth the frequent pain of a deeper self-awareness.

Bibliography

Alexander, F. M. *The use of the self*. New York: Dutton, 1932.

Ames, L. B., and Learned, J. Imaginary companions and related phenomena. *Journal of Genetic Psychology*, 1946, *69*, 147–167.

Antrobus, J. S. The effects of varied and repetitive talking on visual vigilance performance under reduced external stimulation. Unpublished doctoral dissertation, Teachers College, Columbia Univ., 1963.

Antrobus, J. S., Antrobus, Judith S., and Singer, J. L. Eye movements accompanying daydreaming, visual imagery, and thought suppression. *Journal of Abnormal and Social Psychology*, 1964, *69*, 244–252.

Antrobus, J. S., and Singer, J. L. Visual signal detection as a function of sequential variability of simultaneous speech. *Journal of Experimental Psychology*, 1964, *68*, 603–610.

Antrobus, J. S., Singer, J. L., and Greenberg, S. Studies in the stream of consciousness: experimental enhancement and suppression of spontaneous cognitive processes. *Perceptual & Motor Skills*, 1966, *23*, 399–417.

Antrobus, Judith S. Patterns of dreaming and dream recall. Unpublished doctoral dissertation, Teachers College, Columbia Univ., 1962.

Antrobus, Judith S., Dement, W., and Fischer, C. Patterns of dreaming and dream recall. *Journal of Abnormal and Social Psychology*, 1964, *69*, 341–344.

Aserinsky, E., and Kleitman, N. Regularly occurring periods of eye motility, and concomitant phenomena, during sleep. *Science*, 1953, *118*, 273–274.

Atkinson, J. (ed.). *Motives in fantasy, action and society*. Princeton, N.J.: Van Nostrand, 1958.

Bandura, A., Ross, D., and Ross, S. A. Transmission of aggression through imitation of aggressive models. *Journal of Abnormal and Social Psychology*, 1961, *63*, 575–582.

———. Imitation of film-mediated aggressive models. *Journal of Abnormal and Social Psychology*, 1963, *66*, 3–11.

Bandura, A., and Walters, R. H. *Social learning and personality development*. New York: Holt, Rinehart & Winston, 1963.

Barron, F. Threshold for the perception of human movement in inkblots. *Journal of Consulting Psychology*, 1955, *19*, 33–38.

Bartlett, F. M. *Thinking*. New York: Basic Books, 1958.

Basowitz, H., Persky, H., Korchin, S. J., and Grinker, R. R. *Anxiety and stress*. New York: McGraw-Hill, 1955.

Berkowitz, L. The effects of observing violence. *Scientific American*, 1964, *210*, 35–41.

Blank, H. R. The dreams of the blind. *Psychoanalytic Quarterly*, 1958, 27, 158–175.

Brenner, M. S. The relationship between TAT hostility and overt hostile behavior as a function of reported anxiety. Unpublished doctoral dissertation, Teachers College, Columbia Univ., 1960.

Broadbent, D. E. Possibilities and difficulties in the concept of arousal. In D. N. Buckner and J. J. McGrath (eds.), *Vigilance: a symposium*. New York: McGraw-Hill, 1963, pp. 184–198.

Broverman, D. M., Jordan, E. J., Jr., and Phillips, L. Achievement motivation in fantasy and behavior. *Journal of Abnormal and Social Psychology*, 1960, *60*, 374–378.

Buss, A. *The psychology of aggression*. New York: Wiley, 1961.

Cattell, R. B. *Handbook for the IPAT Anxiety Scale*. Champaign, Ill.: Institute for Personality and Ability Testing, 1957.

Colvin, R. W. An experimental analysis of attitudinal determinants underlying behavior to color stimulation in psychoneurotic subjects. Unpublished doctoral dissertation, Duke Univ., 1953.

Cutsforth, T. D. *The blind in school and society*. New York: Appleton, 1933.

Dement, W. The effect of dream deprivation. *Science*, 1960, *131*, 1705–1707.

Dement, W., and Kleitman, N. The relation of eye movements during sleep to dream activity, an objective method for the study of dreaming. *Journal of Experimental Psychology*, 1957, *53*, 339–346.

Dement, W., and Wolpert, E. A. The relation of eye movements, body motility, and external stimuli to dream content.

Journal of Experimental Psychology, 1958, *55*, 543–553.

Deutsch, E. The dream imagery of the blind. *Psychoanalytic Review*, 1928, *15*, 288–293.

Egner, R. E., and Dennon, L. E. (eds.). *The basic writings of Bertrand Russell.* New York: Simon & Schuster, 1962.

Epstein, S. The measurement of drive and conflict in humans: theory and experiment. In M. R. Jones (ed.), *Nebraska Symposium on Motivation.* Lincoln, Neb.: Univ. of Nebraska Press, 1962.

Erikson, E. H. *Childhood and society*, 2nd ed. New York: Norton, 1963.

Estess, B. D. The cathartic effect of two kinds of fantasy aggression on aggressive behavior. Unpublished honors thesis, Smith College, 1960.

Feshbach, S. The drive-reducing function of fantasy behavior. *Journal of Abnormal and Social Psychology*, 1955, *50*, 3–11.

———. The stimulating versus cathartic effects of a vicarious aggressive activity. *Journal of Abnormal and Social Psychology*, 1961, *63*, 169–175.

Fiske, D. W., and Maddi, S. R. (eds.). *Functions of varied experience.* Homewood, Ill.: Dorsey Press, 1961.

Foulkes, D. Dream reports from different stages of sleep. *Journal of Abnormal and Social Psychology*, 1962, *65*, 14–25.

———. Theories of dream formation and recent studies of sleep consciousness. *Psychological Bulletin*, 1964, *62*, 236–247.

Foulkes, D., and Vogel, G. Mental activity at sleep onset. *Journal of Abnormal Psychology*, 1965, *70*, 231–243.

Frazier, E. F. *The black bourgeoisie.* Glencoe, Ill.: Free Press, 1957.

Freud, A. *The ego and the mechanisms of defense.* London: Hogarth, 1937.

Freud, S. Creative writers and daydreaming. In J. Strachey (ed.), *The standard edition of the complete psychological works of Sigmund Freud.* London: Hogarth, 1962a, Vol. IX.

———. Formulations on the two principles of mental functioning. In J. Strachey (ed.), *The standard edition of the complete psychological works of Sigmund Freud.* London: Hogarth, 1962b, Vol. XII.

Fromm, E. *The forgotten language.* New York: Rinehart, 1951.

Galton, F. *Inquiries into the human faculty.* London: Macmillan, 1883.

Gardner, R. W., Holzman, P. S., Klein, G. S., Linton, H. B., and Spence, D. P. Cognitive control: a study of individual consistencies in cognitive behavior. *Psychological Issues,* 1959, *1*, No. 4.

Goldberger, L., and Holt, R. R. A Comparison of isolation effects and their personality correlates in two divergent samples. WADD Technical Report, Wright Air Development Division, Wright Patterson Air Force Base, Ohio, March 1961.

Goldfarb, W. Rorschach test differences between family-reared, institution-reared, and schizophrenic children. *American Journal of Orthopsychiatry,* 1949, *19*, 624–633.

Goldstein, K. *Human nature in the light of psychopathology.* Cambridge, Mass.: Harvard Univ. Press, 1940.

Gordon, W. *Synectics.* New York: Harper, 1961.

Green, G. H. *Psychoanalysis in the classroom.* New York: Putnam, 1922.

———. *The daydream: a study in development.* London: Univ. of London Press, 1923.

Griffiths, R. *Imagination in early childhood.* London: Kegan, Paul, 1935.

Guilford, J. P. Three faces of intellect. *American Psychologist,* 1959, *14*, 469–479.

Hall, G. S. Children's lies. *Pedagogical Seminary,* 1891, *1*, 211–218.

———. *Aspects of child life and education.* Boston: Ginn, 1907.

Hartmann, H. *Ego psychology and the problem of adaptation.* New York: Inter. Univ. Press, 1958.

Hebb, D. O. *The organization of behavior.* New York: Wiley, 1949.

———. The motivating effects of exteroceptive stimulation. *Journal of Mental Science,* 1959, *105*, 235–237.

Helson, R. Childhood interest clusters related to creativity in women. *Journal of Consulting Psychology,* 1965, *29*, 352–361.

Hoffman, F. J. *Freudianism and the literary mind.* New York: Grove Press, 1959.

Holt, R. R. Some reflections on the development of the primary and secondary processes. Unpublished draft report, New York Univ. Research Center for Mental Health, 1960.

———. Imagery: the return of the ostracized. *American Psychologist,* 1964, *19*, 254–264.

Humphrey, R. *Stream of consciousness in the modern novel.* Berkeley: Univ. of California Press, 1958.

Hurlock, E. B., and Burstein, M. The imaginary playmate: a

questionnaire study. *Journal of Genetic Psychology*, 1932, *41*, 380–392.

Huxley, A. *Island*. New York: Bantam; Harper & Row, 1962a.

———. Education on the non-verbal level. *Daedalus*, 1962b, *91*, 279–293.

Isaacs, S. *Social development in young children*. New York: Harcourt, Brace, 1933.

Jaensch, E. R. *Eidetic imagery*. New York: Harcourt, Brace, 1930.

James, W. *The principles of psychology*. New York: Dover Publications, 1950.

Jersild, A. T. *Child psychology*. Englewood Cliffs, N.J.: Prentice-Hall, 1960.

Jersild, A. T., Markey, F. V., and Jersild, C. L. *Children's fears, dreams, wishes, daydreams, likes, dislikes, pleasant and unpleasant memories*. Child Development Monographs, No. 12. New York: Teachers College, Columbia Univ., 1933.

Kagan, J. The measurement of overt aggression from fantasy. *Journal of Abnormal and Social Psychology*, 1956, *52*, 390–393.

Kaplan, N., and Singer, E. Dogmatism and sensory alienation: an empirical investigation. *Journal of Consulting Psychology*, 1963, *27*, 486–491.

Kimmins, C. W. Special features of the teaching of the blind. *Teachers of the Blind*, 1923, *61*, 9–14.

King, G. F. An interpersonal conception of Rorschach human movement and delusional content. *Journal of Projective Techniques*, 1960, *24*, 161–163.

Kleitman, N. *Sleep and wakefulness*. Chicago: Univ. of Chicago Press, 1963.

Korchin, S. J. Anxiety and cognition. In C. Scheerer (ed.), *Cognition: theory, research, and promise*. New York: Harper & Row, 1964.

Lair, W. S. The psychoanalytic theory of identification. Unpublished doctoral dissertation, Harvard Univ., 1949.

Leiman, A. H., and Epstein, S. Thematic sexual responses as related to sexual drive and guilt. *Journal of Abnormal and Social Psychology*, 1961, *63*, 169–175.

Lesser, L. An experimental study of the drive-reducing function of imagination and fantasy in young children. Unpublished doctoral dissertation, New York Univ., 1962.

Lewin, K. Behavior and development as a function of the total situation. In L. Carmichael (ed.), *Manual of Child Psychology*. New York: Wiley, 1946.

Lindner, R. *The fifty-minute hour*. New York: Holt, Rinehart, & Winston, 1955.

Luborsky, L., Blinder, B., and Mackworth, N. Eye fixation and recall of pictures as a function of GSR responsivity. *Perceptual and Motor Skills*, 1963, *16*, 469–483, Monogr. Supplements, 5–V16.

Markey, F. V. *Imaginative behavior in preschool children*. Child Development Monographs, No. 18. New York: Teachers College, Columbia Univ., 1935.

McArthur, C. C. Personality differences between middle and upper classes. *Journal of Abnormal and Social Psychology*, 1955, *50*, 247–254.

McCartney, F. M. A comparative study of the dreams of the blind and of the sighted with special reference to Freud's theory. Unpublished M.A. thesis, Indiana Univ., 1913.

McClelland, D. C. *The achieving society*. Princeton, N.J.: Van Nostrand, 1961.

McClelland, D. C., Atkinson, J. W., Clark, R. A., and Lowell, E. L. *The achievement motive*. New York: Appleton-Century, 1953.

McCurdy, H. G. The childhood pattern of genius. *Horizon*, 1960, *2*, 32–38.

McGrath, J. J. Irrelevant stimulation and vigilance performance. In D. N. Buckner, and J. J. McGrath (eds.), *Vigilance: a symposium*. New York: McGraw-Hill, 1963.

McKellar, P. *Imagination and thinking*. New York: Basic Books, 1957.

Meltzoff, J., Singer, J. L., and Korchin, S. J. Motor inhibition and Rorschach movement responses: a test of sensory-tonic theory. *Journal of Personality*, 1953, *21*, 400–410.

Mintz, A. Schizophrenic speech and sleepy speech. *Journal of Abnormal and Social Psychology*, 1948, *43*, 548–549.

Mischel, W. Research and theory on delay of gratification. In B. A. Maher (ed.), *Progress in experimental personality research*, Vol. 2. Garden City, N. Y.: Academic Press, 1965.

Mowrer, O. H. *Learning theory and behavior*. New York: Wiley, 1960.

Murphy, G. *Personality: a biosocial approach*. New York: Harper, 1947.

Murphy, G., Murphy, L., and Newcomb, T. *Experimental social psychology*. New York: Harper, 1937.

Murray, H. *Explorations in personality*. New York: Oxford Univ. Press, 1938.

Mussen, P., and Rutherford, E. Effects of aggressive cartoons on children's aggressive play. *Journal of Abnormal and Social Psychology*, 1961, *62*, 461–464.

Opler, M. K., and Singer, J. L. Ethnic differences in behavior and psychopathology. *International Journal of Social Psychiatry*, 1956, *2*, 11–22.

Oswald, I. *Sleeping and waking*. New York: Elsevier, 1962.

Page, H. A. Studies in fantasy: daydreaming and the TAT. *American Psychologist*, 1956, *11*, 392.

———. Studies in fantasy—daydreaming frequency and Rorschach scoring categories. *Journal of Consulting Psychology*, 1957, *21*, 111–114.

Palmer, J. O. Attitudinal correlates of Rorschach's experience-balance. *Journal of Projective Techniques*, 1956, *19*, 138–145.

Piaget, J. *The language and thought of the child*. New York: Harcourt, Brace, 1932.

———. *Play, dreams and imitation in childhood*. New York: Norton, 1962.

Pytkowicz, A. R. An experimental study of the reduction of hostility through phantasy. Unpublished doctoral dissertation, Univ. of Washington, 1963.

Rapaport, D. *Organization and pathology of thought*. New York: Columbia Univ. Press, 1951.

Rapaport, D., Gill, M., and Shafer, R. *Diagnostic psychological testing*, Vol. 2, Chicago: Year Book Publishers, 1946.

Reik, T. *Of love and lust*. New York: Grove Press, 1959.

Rickers-Ovsiankina, M. R. (ed.). *Rorschach psychology*. New York: Wiley, 1960.

Riess, A. A study of some genetic behavioral correlates of human movement responses in children's Rorschach protocols. Unpublished doctoral dissertation, New York Univ., 1957.

Roe, A. *The making of a scientist*. New York: Dodd, Mead, 1952.

Roffwarg, H. P., Dement, W. C., Muzio, J. N., and Fisher, C. Dream imagery: relationship to rapid eye movements of sleep. *AMA Archives of General Psychiatry*, 1962, 7, 235–258.

Rorschach, H. *Psychodiagnostics*. Berne: Hans Huber, 1942.

Rowe, R. R. The effects of daydreaming under stress. Unpublished doctoral dissertation, Teachers College, Columbia Univ., 1963.

Rowley, J. M. The imagination of the blind. *Beacon,* 1922, *66,* 7–9.

Sarason, S. B. Projective techniques in mental deficiency. *Journal of Personality,* 1944, *13,* 237–245.

Saxton, G. Spontaneous fantasy as a resource of high grade retardates for coping with a failure-stress situation. *Journal of Abnormal and Social Psychology,* 1962, *64,* 81–84.

Schachtel, E. *Metamorphosis.* New York: Basic Books, 1959.

Schachter, S. *The psychology of affiliation.* Stanford, Cal.: Stanford Univ. Press, 1959.

Schachter, S., and Singer, J. E. Cognitive, social, and physiological determinants of emotional state. *Psychological Review,* 1962, *69,* 379–399.

Schonbar, R. Some manifest characteristics of recallers and non-recallers of dreams. *Journal of Consulting Psychology,* 1959, *23,* 414–418.

Seeman, W. The Freudian theory of daydreams: an operational analysis. *Psychological Bulletin,* 1951, *48,* 369–382.

Shaffer, L. F. *The psychology of adjustment.* Boston: Houghton-Mifflin, 1936.

Sharaf, M. R. An approach to the theory and measurement of introception. Unpublished doctoral dissertation, Harvard Univ., 1959.

Sherman, M. *Mental hygiene and education.* New York: Longmans, Green, 1934.

Silberer, H. Report on a method of eliciting and observing certain symbolic hallucination phenomena. In D. Rapaport (ed.), *Organization and pathology of thought.* New York: Columbia Univ. Press, 1951.

Singer, J. L. Delayed gratification and ego-development: implications for clinical and experimental research. *Journal of Consulting Psychology,* 1955, *19,* 259–266.

———. The experience type: some behavioral correlates and theoretical implications. In M. R. Rickers-Ovsiankina (ed.), *Rorschach psychology.* New York: Wiley, 1960.

———. Imagination and waiting ability in young children. *Journal of Personality,* 1961, *29,* 396–413.

Singer, J. L., and Antrobus, J. S. A factor-analytic study of daydreaming and conceptually-related cognitive and personality variables. *Perceptual and Motor Skills.* Monograph Supplement 3–V17, 1963.

———. Eye movements during fantasies. *AMA Archives of General Psychiatry,* 1965, *12,* 71–76.

Singer, J. L., and Chipman, A. The generalization of imaginative learning to delaying capacity in children. Draft report submitted to NIMH under Grant M–2279, "Dimensions of Fantasy and Imagination, " 1961.

Singer, J. L., and McCraven, V. Some characteristics of adult daydreaming. *Journal of Psychology*, 1961, *51*, 151–164.

———. Patterns of daydreaming in American subcultural groups. *International Journal of Social Psychiatry*, 1962, *8*, 272–282.

Singer, J. L., Meltzoff, J., and Goldman, G. D. Rorschach movement responses following motor inhibition and hyperactivity. *Journal of Consulting Psychology*, 1952, *16*, 359–364.

Singer, J. L., and Opler, M. K. Contrasting patterns of fantasy and motility in Irish and Italian schizophrenics. *Journal of Abnormal and Social Psychology*, 1956, *53*, 42–47.

Singer, J. L., and Rowe, R. An experimental study of some relationships between daydreaming and anxiety. *Journal of Consulting Psychology*, 1962, *26*, 446–454.

Singer, J. L., and Schonbar, R. Correlates of daydreaming: a dimension of self-awareness. *Journal of Consulting Psychology*, 1961, *25*, 1–6.

Singer, J. L., and Spohn, H. Some behavioral correlates of Rorschach's experience type. *Journal of Consulting Psychology*, 1954, *18*, 1–9.

———. The response of schizophrenic patients to a televised World Series game: a study in social isolation. *Journal of Abnormal and Social Psychology*, 1956, *53*, 375–377.

Singer, J. L., and Streiner, B. Imaginative content in the dream and fantasy play of blind and sighted children. *Perceptual and Motor Skills*, in press, 1966.

Singer, J. L., and Sugarman, D. Some Thematic Apperception Test correlates of Rorschach human movement responses. *Journal of Consulting Psychology*, 1955, *19*, 117–119.

Singer, J. L., Wilensky, H., and McCraven, V. Delaying capacity, fantasy, and planning ability: a factorial study of some basic ego functions. *Journal of Consulting Psychology*, 1956, *20*, 375–383.

Smith, T. Psychology of daydreaming. *American Journal of Psychology*, 1904, *15*, 465–488.

Snow, C. P. *The two cultures and the scientific revolution*. New York: Cambridge Univ. Press, 1959.

Solomon, P., Kubzansky, P. E., and Leiderman, P. H. (eds.). *Sensory deprivation*. Cambridge, Mass.: Harvard Univ. Press, 1961.

Spivack, G. Some cognitive deficiencies in poorly self-controlled adolescents. Paper presented at Meetings of the American Psychological Association, Los Angeles, 1964.

Spivack, G., and Levine, M. *Self-regulation and acting-out in normal adolescents.* Progress Report for National Institutes of Mental Health, Grant M–4531. Devon, Penn.: Devereaux Foundation, 1964.

Stein, M., and Heinze, S. *Creativity and the individual.* Glencoe, Ill.: Free Press, 1960.

Strodtbeck, F. L. Family interaction, values, and achievement. In D. C. McClelland, A. L. Baldwin, U. Bronfenbrenner, and F. L. Strodtbeck. *Talent and Society.* Princeton, N.J.: Van Nostrand, 1958.

Sullivan, H. S. *Clinical studies in psychiatry.* New York: Norton, 1953*a*.

———. *The interpersonal theory of psychiatry.* New York: Norton, 1953*b*.

Symonds, P. M. *Adolescent fantasy.* New York: Columbia Univ. Press, 1949.

Symonds, P. M., and Jensen, A. R. *From adolescent to adult.* New York: Columbia Univ. Press, 1961.

Tart, C. Frequency of dream recall and some personality measures. *Journal of Consulting Psychology,* 1962, *26*, 467–470.

Tauber, E. S., and Green, M. *Prelogical experience.* New York: Basic Books, 1959.

Temerlin, M. K. One determinant of the capacity to free-associate in psychotherapy. *Journal of Abnormal and Social Psychology,* 1956, *53*, 16–18.

Tomkins, S. *Affect, imagery, consciousness,* Vol. 1. New York: Springer, 1962.

Tomkins, S., and Messick, S. (eds.). *Computer simulation of personality.* New York: Wiley, 1963.

Ullman, M. Dreams and arousal. *American Journal of Psychotherapy,* 1958, *12*, 222–233.

Varendonck, J. *The psychology of daydreams.* New York: Macmillan, 1921.

Vostrovsky, C. Study of imaginary companions. *Education,* 1894, *15*, 393–398.

Wagner, N., and Stegemann, K. Does the schizoid child develop into an adult schizophrenic? Empirical data. Unpublished report submitted in connection with State of Washington Grant 171, "Imagination and Impulse Control in Children," 1964.

Weisskopf, E. A. A transcendence index as a proposed measure in the TAT. *Journal of Psychology*, 1950, *29*, 379–390.

Welsh, G. S. Factor dimensions A and R. In G. S. Welsh and W. G. Dahlstrom (eds.), *Basic readings on the MMPI in psychology and medicine*. Minneapolis: Univ. of Minnesota Press, 1956.

Werner, H. Motion and motion perception: a study on vicarious perception. *Journal of Psychology*, 1945, *19*, 317–327.

——. *The comparative psychology of mental development*. Chicago: Follett, 1948.

Werner, H., and Wapner, S. Toward a general theory of perception. *Psychological Review*, 1952, *59*, 324–333.

West, L. J. (ed.). *Hallucinations*. New York: Grune & Stratton, 1962.

Wexler, D., Mendelson, J., Leiderman, P. H., and Solomon, P. Sensory deprivation: a technique for studying psychiatric aspects of stress. *AMA Archives of Neurology and Psychiatry*, 1958, 79, 225–233.

White, R. W. Motivation reconsidered: the concept of competence. *Psychological Review*, 1959, *66*, 297–333.

——. Ego and reality in psychoanalytic theory. *Psychological Issues*, 1964, *3*, Monograph 11.

Witkin, H. A., Dyk, R. B., Patterson, H. F., Goodenough, D. R., and Karp, S. A. *Psychological differentiation*. New York: Wiley, 1962.

Wittkower, E. *A psychiatrist looks at tuberculosis*. London: National Association for the Prevention of Tuberculosis, 1949.

Woods, Sister F. J. *Cultural values of American ethnic groups*. New York: Harper, 1956.

Wyatt, S., and Fraser, J. A. *The effects of monotony in work.* "Great Britian Industrial Fatigue Research Board Reports," 1929, No. 56.

INDEX